The Remarkable Career of
Jack Reeder
Engineering Test Pilot

MARK CHAMBERS

HIGH TIDE PUBLICATIONS
DELTAVILLE, VIRGINIA

Copyright © 2016 Mark Chambers

All rights reserved. No part of this publication may be reproduced, distributed or transmitted in any form or by any means, including photocopying, recording, or other electronic or mechanical methods, without the prior written permission of the publisher, except in the case of brief quotations embodied in critical reviews and certain other noncommercial uses permitted by copyright law. For permission requests, write to the publisher, addressed "Attention: Permissions Coordinator," at the address below.

High Tide Publications, Inc.
1000 Bland Point Road
Deltaville, Virginia 23043
www.HighTidePublications.com

Ordering Information: Quantity sales. Special discounts are available on quantity purchases by corporations, associations, and others. For details, contact the "Special Sales Department" at the address above.

The Remarkable Career of Jack Reeder, Engineering Test Pilot/2nd ed.

Printed in the United States of America

ISBN 978-0692744826

Table of Contents

FOREWORD	I
PREFACE	III
ACKNOWLEDGEMENTS	V
CHAPTER ONE - THE LEGEND BEINGS	1
CHAPTER TWO - IN THE CAVE OF THE WINDS	13
CHAPTER THREE - A CAREER TAKES FLIGHT	39
CHAPTER FOUR - THE JET AGE	75
CHAPTER FIVE - WHIRLY BIRDS	109
CHAPTER SIX - BIG GUYS AND LITTLE GUYS	137
CHAPTER SEVEN - THE V/STOL CHALLENGE	161
CHAPTER EIGHT - THE FUTURE OF AIR TRANSPORTATION: THE TERMINAL CONFIGURED VEHICLE PROGRAM	191
CHAPTER NINE - JACK REEDER'S LEGACY	205
Appendices	219

 A - Airplanes and Rotorcraft Piloted by Jack Reeder
 B - Bibliography of Jack Reeder's Published Papers
 C - Awards and Professional Association Memberships

ABOUT THE AUTHOR	241

Foreword

I'm honored by this opportunity to say some words about my old friend and mentor, Jack Reeder. Jack hired me into the NASA in 1966; as a NASA research pilot, I worked for and with him at the Langley Research Center for 14 years, until he retired in 1980. I was Head of Flight Operations and Chief Test Pilot at NASA Langley from 1968 to 1987. Beside our professional association, my wife and I were close social friends with Jack and Frances.

Jack had such stature in the field of flight test that all of us in the pilots' office felt very fortunate to be working with him. He invited opposing opinions in professional discussions…provided, of course, that the opposition was factually based. If that were so, he would listen, and I've known him to change his original idea, a high mark for any manager, and one that always gains respect from employees. Well, he had that, in spades.

I guess my main memory of Jack is of his unswerving dedication to Truth, which is what flight testing is all about. His wry, self-deprecatory manner would sometimes come out like, "Dammit! I screwed that all up!". But that never happened, to my knowledge. His deft, sure touch with an aircraft, coupled with a bright, analytical mind, made him an exceptional test pilot. During 46 years in flight testing, I never knew his equal as a flying qualities test pilot and analyst. It wasn't just having good hands, it was being able to mentally dissect what he had just seen and done and report it in clear engineering terms. To me that's the classic definition of a test pilot, what all of us would want to be.

Also, I never knew anyone in the business with as wide and diversified a group of friends and admirers as Jack. Among those that I was aware of were the people at the Flight Safety Foundation, VADM Forrest Peterson, USN, several key people at the Royal Aeronautical Establishment, U.K.,

NASA Ames and Dryden, Sikorsky, Lockheed, and of course many others, all key engineering and flight people.

Jack became NACA's first helicopter pilot in 1944 and played a prime role in the development of the first rotorcraft flight standards. Finally, some of his major contri-butions lay in foresight, what the aeronautical world would need next, both civil and military. His advocacy brought the Boeing experimental 737 airplane to Langley to investigate the coming need for a link between air traffic control and airplane infor-mation and control systems of the future. On the military side, he was responsible for bringing the Hawker-Siddeley Kestrel VTOL fighter prototype to the Langley han-gar, resulting in pioneering combat inflight thrust vectoring investigations, an arrow now in the quiver of most modern fighters.

I'm glad I knew Jack Reeder, as a test pilot and as a friend.

Jim Patton

Jim Patton received national recognition for his role as chief pilot in the program when he received the Iven C. Kincheloe Award of the Society of Experimental Test Pilots in 1978

Preface

The late John P. "Jack" Reeder is widely acknowledged within the international aeronautical community as one of the world's outstanding engineering test pilots. His drive and passion for helping aircraft designers to produce superior military aircraft and efficient, safe civil aircraft set him aside from other research and company test pilots, and earned him the respect and awe of his peers and friends. Jack quickly put his formal college education in aeronautical engineering to work, building an appreciation of the complex factors that govern the performance and flying qualities of airplanes. Making the remarkable transition from wind-tunnel engineer to test pilot, he was able to communicate and analyze topics from both perspectives, thereby providing a unique translation of jargon and engineering analysis between the two groups. The immediate impact of his efforts was to help and guide subordinate pilots in understanding and mastering new flight-test methods and the interpretation of aircraft behavior; while emphasizing the value of the pilot's assessments to the engineering staff. Most importantly, Jack accomplished this while maintaining an unassuming attitude without arrogance or self-gratification through exposure to the media. Like most of the NACA/NASA test pilots at the Langley Research Center, Jack assumed the attitude that he was "just doing his job" when it came to perfecting flight concepts or making important refinements to aircraft/rotorcraft designs. His uncanny ability to apply his aeronautical engineering expertise within the cockpit made him a "go to guy" when the military services or industry officials turned to the NACA or NASA for flight-testing advice or assessments. He was truly a national asset who made numerous contributions that furthered the state of the art in aircraft design and technology.

It is a tremendous honor to have had the opportunity to interview Jack

Reeder on many occasions and to write about the extraordinary life and career of this pioneering icon in American aviation history. The author had the pleasure of not only associating with him for historical interests but more importantly as a good friend. Over the last decade of his life, we enjoyed endless conversations concerning flight research and his personal anecdotes of his experiences at NACA/NASA Langley. Jack's vivid and riveting recollections of his early flying experiences only sharpened as he aged, and his stories will never be forgotten by me and his many friends. The author will never forget working in NASA Langley's Office of External Affairs one summer afternoon in 1994, when Reeder, then age 78, made a special trip to discuss and deliver his personal materials regarding supersonic propeller flight research as a gift to the author. It has also been an honor to have the opportunity to interview his family members and many of his technical peers and admirers.

I am eternally grateful to Jack and his family for sharing their extensive collection of photographs and documents. Many of these items are unpublished, anecdotal, and extremely revealing regarding his personal and frank assessments of advanced aircraft and rotorcraft. Through extensive research and personal interviews of Jack, his family, and his close associates, an overwhelming amount of his notes, comments, reports, and personal material was collected and interwoven into this highly intriguing personal story. It is hoped that the reader will be equally impressed by the achievements of this remarkable man. Although the focus of new generations of airplane enthusiasts may be directed toward the flamboyant reputations of other famous test pilots, the objective of this book is to expose them to this remarkable man and maintain the legacy of his contributions and personal character.

Acknowledgements

The author wishes to thank numerous contributors to this publication, especially the family of Jack Reeder. Mrs. Frances Winder Reeder and their daughter, Shirley Reeder Randall, provided delightful and informative interviews, which greatly expanded my knowledge of Jack's unique character, interests, and relationships. Many of the factors that drove Jack's career choices and his family life were also covered in detail. The special bonds that held the Reeder family together were evident throughout the interviews, and the author is deeply indebted to the family for their assistance.

Sincere thanks go to several active and retired personnel of the National Advisory Committee for Aeronautics (NACA) and the National Aeronautics and Space Administration (NASA). These individuals included Jack Reeder's engineering and piloting peers, subordinates and friends, and technical archivists and photographic experts. Special thanks go to Mr. Keith Loftin, son of the late Mr. Laurence K. "Larry" Loftin, Jr., former Director for Aeronautics at the NASA Langley Research Center, for his interest and efforts in documenting the history of flight research at NACA/NASA Langley, and his extraordinary help in providing materials defining the career of one of the most unheralded national heroes in aeronautical research, Jack Reeder. Larry Loftin began his professional career as an aeronautical engineer at the NACA Langley Memorial Aeronautical Laboratory in 1944. He specialized in research in the areas of aerodynamics and aero elasticity, and retired following a distinguished 30-year career, during which he was internationally recognized for his personal expertise and capabilities as a senior manager of research. Throughout his career, Loftin was a very close friend of Jack Reeder, working with day-to-day contact on numerous flight research programs — even flying together in sport aircraft in their spare time. Loftin authored a plethora of aeronautical technical papers, and before passing away in 2003, he had begun to write a book about Jack Reeder's contributions as a tribute to his close friend. The author is eternally grateful to Keith Loftin for providing his father's unpublished and unfinished manuscript entitled "A Research Pilot's World as Seen from the Cockpit of a NASA Engineer-Pilot", which provided a rich source of information for this book. Keith also contributed his father's extensive library of historic aircraft/personnel photographs and many important documents on flight research at NACA/NASA Langley. In addition to honoring the memory of Jack Reeder, this work is devoted to completing the manuscript begun by Larry Loftin.

Current and former staff members of Langley were especially helpful in preparing this document. Jack's engineering and piloting peers and subordinates provided interviews that covered personal perspectives on his accomplishments, anecdotal experiences, and often emotional viewpoints on his personal standards and ambitions. Special thanks to retired Langley pilot Lee H. Person, Jr., who Jack groomed into one of Langley's most respected research pilots. Lee's close relationship and interactions with Jack provided unique and valuable insights into Jack's mentoring and management skills. W. Hewitt Phillips and Thomas Toll provided comments on the flight test activities and culture at Langley, and objectives and results of specific airplane investigations involving Reeder. Thanks also to Todd Hodges, who shared information gathered in his close personal friendship with Jack, including technical reports, photographs, and other information. Todd was a notable contributor to this material, driven by a common desire to ensure that Jack Reeder is given appropriate credit in the history of flight. In addition to his contributions for fixed-wing aircraft, Jack's contributions to rotorcraft and V/STOL technology stand out in his long list of accomplishments. The author thanks notable NASA rotorcraft experts Frederick Gustafson, Robert J. Tapscott, Robert Huston, and John Garren for their assistance in preparing this document as well as Mr. John Paulson for sharing his photographic slides of various aircraft and rotorcraft.

The author also thanks A. G. "Gary" Price, retired Head of NASA Langley Research Center Office of External Affairs, for providing access to interview transcripts and historical articles. Thanks also go to Gail Langevin, NASA Langley Research Center Office of External Affairs, and her Langley Aerospace Research Summer Scholars (LARSS) student Torey William Boykin who provided access to and assistance with locating flight-test reports and historical anecdotes found in the NASA Langley Research Center Historical Archives. Special thanks also go to the staff of the Langley Photographic Laboratory for assisting in photographic reproduction, Pat West (NASA Langley) for data and administrative assistance, and Barbara Trippe of the NASA Langley Flight Operations Office for providing access to historical photos and official pilot information. Garland Gouger and the staff of the Langley Technical Library provided invaluable assistance in locating reports and other documents. Finally, the author would like to thank his father, Langley retiree Joseph R. Chambers, for serving as technical consultant.

In July 1930, Jack Reeder (visible at lower left), who was 14 years old at the time, flew for the first time as a passenger in an airplane at a flying field in his home town of Houghton, Michigan. The airplane, a five seat New Standard D-25 was powered by a 220 horse-power Wright J-5 engine and was operated by the Gates Flying Circus (part of the Gates-Day Aircraft Corporation).
Jack Reeder via NASA Langley Research Center

Chapter One
The Legend Begins

John P. "Jack" Reeder

NASA Langley Research Center

He witnessed, first hand, the accelerated evolution of flight from the pioneering days of fabric covered biplanes to today's sophisticated high-performance military and civil jet aircraft. Along the way, he had the opportunity to fly and evaluate some of the most exotic aircraft in the world. He correctly anticipated emerging challenges to the modern civil air transportation system, and he formulated and managed critical research in airspace operations and terminal-area capabilities to provide solutions to evolving problems. He participated in critical national projects as a highly respected test pilot, while using his sharp engineering knowledge and perspectives to communicate with pilots and engineers. His research travels took him to worldwide destinations, and throughout his career he befriended some of the most famous and intriguing personalities in the aviation community. He was a simple man by today's standards – highly devoted to his wife and family, always placing their needs above his work, loved his job, and foremost was rather unassuming about his potentially hazardous occupation. When he contributed to significant milestones in aeronautical research, he never bragged or exhibited the arrogance that all too often were characteristic of famous figures in the aviation world. Instead, he thought he was just doing his job, and would have no part of any elaborate headline-grabbing celebrations. However, the life of John P. "Jack" Reeder was anything but mundane – it was an extraordinary adventure and lesson in human excellence.

Jack Reeder was born on May 27, 1916 in Houghton, Michigan, an area of the Keweenaw Peninsula that became known as "Copper Country". In 1923, his father, John Harry Reeder, who worked as a mining engineer, moved his wife, Mary Margaret Roehm Reeder, daughter Mary, and son Jack to Sudbury, Ontario, to pursue a temporary work assignment. There, young Jack gained his first inspirations for flight and love of aircraft by watching vintage World War I Curtiss HS-2L flying boats performing low-altitude, forest-fire patrols. The HS-2L flying boats made their debut patrolling against enemy submarines during the last two years of World War I, and the United States Navy flew them on antisubmarine duty off the East Coast from bases in Nova Scotia. When the war was over, the Navy donated twelve of the planes to Canada. In 1919, the first HS-2Ls went into Canadian civil use in Québec forestry work, remaining the primary Canadian bush aircraft until the mid-1920s. Young Jack took great delight whenever the observer, seated in the gunner's position in the front of the aircraft, waved to him.

The Curtiss HS-2LS, flown by the Canadian forestry service, served as Jack Reeder's source of inspiration for aviation during his early youth.
Martin Copp via Larry Loftin

In 1924, the Reeder family moved back to the Upper Peninsula of Michigan, making the town of Stambaugh, located in "Iron Country", their home. Unfortunately, there was no aviation-related activity in the skies over Stambaugh during the 1920's to stimulate Jack's interests. Instead, reading popular aeronautical-related literature of the day fueled his enthusiasm for aviation. "Books like *We* by Charles A. Lindbergh, *The Red Knight of Germany* by Floyd Gibbons and *War Birds, Diary of an Unknown Aviator*, as well as the numerous pulp magazines like *Flying Aces*, *War Birds* and *Wings*, which dealt with fictional adventures of World War I aviators, were devoured with enthusiasm. Books on how to fly, such as the classic *Stick and Rudder* by *Wolfgang Langewiesche*, as well as later books on flying by *Assen Jordnoff* were studied with intense interest."[1]

Jack also nourished an intense interest in building and flying model airplanes, especially models of World War I legendary fighters such as the Fokker D-7 and Spad XIII. In July 1930, he gained his first actual flying experience when he flew as a passenger aboard a New Standard model D-25 biplane. The airplane featured five seats, positioned in an open-cockpit arrangement. "The aircraft had accommodations for four passengers in the front cockpit, seated in two rows of two each, with the pilot in a single cockpit located behind the passengers. Jack recalled that on his first flight both of the front two seats were needed for a very large young woman, while he and his friend sat in the two rear seats."

After advancing to Stambaugh High School, Jack formulated a plan for his career – enroll in a collegiate aeronautical engineering program and study engineering, then enlist in the U.S. Navy for flight training, and ultimately advance to the position of experimental test pilot. While he was in high school, Jack also maintained an interest in athletics and played football, serving as an end on the 1933 Upper Peninsula championship football team.

The University of Michigan

In September 1934, Jack attended the University of Michigan to begin studies in aeronautical engineering. In addition to being one of the most prestigious institutions for higher education in the United States, the University of Michigan had the distinction of being the first collegiate institution in the country to offer a degree course in aeronautical engineering, and was also one of the first colleges in the country to develop a degree curriculum in aeronautical engineering. "Aeronautical engineering was considered by many to be somewhat esoteric if not downright frivolous at the time. The school of Aeronautical Engineering had the advantage of operating with an endowment from the *Daniel Guggenheim Fund for the Promotion of Aeronautics*.

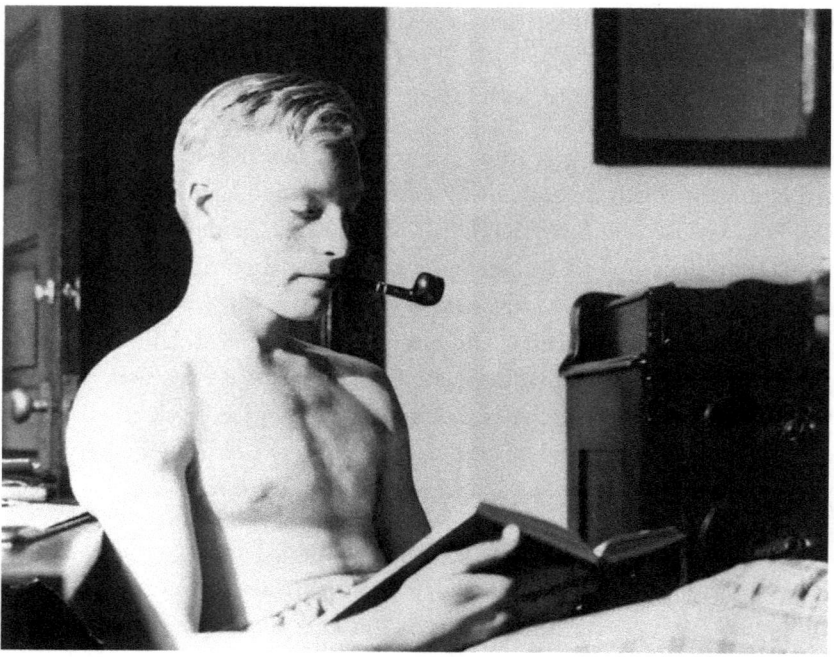

Engaged in studies while a freshman at the University of Michigan in Ann Arbor.

Jack Reeder via NASA Langley Research Center

A total of eight institutions of higher learning were so endowed; these contributions by the Guggenheim Fund had an important and lasting influence on the development of aeronautics in the United States."[3] Jack began his studies under several prominent professors including Professor Felix Pawlowski, a critical figure in the development of the University's Aeronautical Engineering Department in 1916; Professor Edward Stalker,

Department Head; and notable graduate student instructors such as Willis Hawkins and Rudy Thoren. These instructors later advanced to positions of distinguished leadership within the Lockheed Corporation.

In his junior Year at the University of Michigan, he soloed in a Franklin Glider in 1936.

Jack Reeder via NASA Langley Research Center

"In the 1930's, the first two years in an Aeronautical Engineering curriculum usually consisted of basic engineering courses such as Physics, Chemistry, Mathematics, Drawing, Thermodynamics, Mechanics, and English. Specialization was reserved for the last two years, in which such courses as Aerodynamics, Stability and Control, Propulsion Systems, Structures, and Airplane Design were taught. Various laboratory courses, including an Aerodynamics Laboratory which was equipped with an 8-ft. wind tunnel capable of speeds of 200 miles per hour, were an integral part of the course of study."[4]

When he was a Junior at University of Michigan, Jack became a member of the University Glider Club and successfully performed his first solo flight in an aircraft, a Franklin glider, in 1936.

Jack later recalled his experience in a conversation with Laurence K. Loftin:

> *I had read a great deal about flying airplanes and knew how the controls functioned. However, I had also steered a bobsled with my feet during the winters in the Upper Peninsula. On my first glider tow (by truck), after having been cautioned to hold the stick forward to stay on the ground, I found my habit from bobsled experience overcoming book knowledge, and in trying to cope with my misuse of the rudder, I found myself airborne. After a moment of shock, I released the towline, held the rudder fixed, and landed straight ahead using a little back-stick to ease the landing. At any rate, I banished any potential fright of soloing in a hurry.*[5]
>
> *In the final year, each student was required to prepare the preliminary design of a new airplane. Jack's senior project design was for a five-place, low-wing monoplane, equipped with a 450 horsepower engine and a retractable landing gear. The design was somewhat like the very advanced Spartan Executive which appeared on the market at about that time.*[6]

Jack graduated from the University of Michigan in the highest ranking tier of his class. "His election to *Tau Beta Pi*, the honorary engineering society (equivalent to *Phi Beta Kappa* in the Arts and Sciences), attested to his high academic standing, as well as the fact that he was allowed to graduate in the class of 1938 with a degree in Aeronautical Engineering without taking his final examinations."[7]

After graduation, a National Advisory Committee for Aeronautics (NACA) Langley Memorial Aeronautical Laboratory (LMAL) recruiter, who also happened to be a graduate of the University of Michigan, recruited Jack. Jack was offered a position as an aeronautical engineer working in the LMAL 30 x 60 ft. Full Scale Wind Tunnel at Langley Field, in Hampton, Virginia, in the spring of 1938. The LMAL was the first civilian government research laboratory devoted to the study of aeronautics in the United States and its research projects had led to international recognition and prestige. Jack's family was strongly in favor of Jack accepting the position with the NACA. Buoyed by their support and the advice of his university professors, Jack accepted the position and decided to postpone his plan to enter the Navy's flight training program. This decision would ultimately work out better for Jack because he subsequently flew not only Navy aircraft and rotorcraft, but aircraft and rotorcraft from all branches of the military services, in addition to civil transports and light or general aviation (GA) aircraft.

Jack and two of his classmates from University of Michigan, Norman Land and Ralph Ulmer, who also accepted jobs at NACA Langley, packed their personal belongings into Ralph's car and made the long journey from Michigan down to Hampton. Jack took up residence in a housing complex, located on Chesapeake Avenue in Hampton, that became known as "the X-Club" with several of his NACA coworkers and went to work at Langley for Elton Miller, Chief of Aerodynamics.

Jack Reeder (left) and classmates in graduation attire following graduation ceremony at University of Michigan, June 1938.

(Jack Reeder via NASA Langley Research Center)

Jack Reeder's housemates and fellow NACA engineers at the "X-Club" in Hampton, Virginia. From left to right: Blake Carson, Maury White, Al Young, and Gene Wasielewski (in chair).

Jack Reeder via NASA Langley Research Center

Chapter One Notes

1. Loftin, Laurence K., Jr. (Unpublished Manuscript, July 1986). <u>A Research Pilot's World As Seen From The Cockpit Of A NASA Engineer-Pilot</u>, Chap. 2, p.1.

2. Ibid, Chap.2, p. 2

3. Ibid., Chap. 2, p. 3, also found in Hallion Richard P. *Legacy of Flight, The Guggenheim Contribution to American Aviation,* University of Washington Press, Seattle and London, 1977.

4. Loftin, Laurence K., Jr. (Unpublished Manuscript, July 1986) <u>A Research Pilot's World As Seen From The Cockpit Of A NASA Engineer-Pilot</u>, Chap. 2, p.3.

5. Ibid., Chap. 2, p.4.

6. Ibid, Chap. 2, p. 3.

7. Ibid, Chap. 2, p. 4.

In April 1938, the NACA began Full Scale Wind Tunnel studies to reduce the aerodynamic drag of the Brewster XF2A-1 Buffalo fighter design.

NASA Langley Research Center via Larry Loftin

Chapter Two
In the Cave of the Winds

When Jack Reeder began his work with the NACA, the precursor to today's National Aeronautics and Space Administration (NASA), at the LMAL, in 1938, the Laboratory employed a staff of about 500 people. This number included engineers, administrative staffers, mechanics and machinists, and wind-tunnel technicians and model makers. What started out as a modest research laboratory operation in 1919 had burgeoned into a premier aeronautical research establishment by 1938. At that time, LMAL possessed several wind tunnels, two seaplane tow tanks for testing the hydrodynamic performance of seaplane hulls and wing floats, a structures laboratory for testing various aircraft materials, and a flight research hangar to house and perform calibrations and maintenance on the lab's flight research aircraft.

The Full Scale Tunnel

When Jack first arrived at Langley, he expressed an interest in working in the Flight Research Division. The Flight Research Division already had a full complement of research pilots. He was assigned to the Full Scale Tunnel Section as there was a pressing need for more professionals with aeronautical engineering educational backgrounds at the Full Scale Tunnel facility.

The monstrous Full Scale Tunnel at Langley was an open-throat design that featured a test section having dimensions of 30-feet high by 60-feet wide, using two four-bladed 35.5-ft diameter propellers driven by two electric 4000 horsepower motors. The tunnel, which became operational in 1931, was capable of providing a top speed of nearly 100 miles per hour. The tunnel was originally constructed for performing research on full-scale aircraft of the period as well as large powered models. Over the years,

Above: The original XP-39 during tests in the Langley Full Scale Tunnel in August 1939.

Below: A second series of "drag cleanup" studies on the XP-39, re-designated as the XP-39B, were conducted by Jack Reeder in the Langley Full Scale Tunnel.

NASA Langley Research Center

the Langley Full Scale Tunnel would function as a vital tool in defining fundamental aerodynamic data for designers as well as testing advanced aircraft and spacecraft. This remarkable facility has been in operation for over 75 years. Its research results have proven to be so vital to the nation's progress and position of international leadership in the field of aerospace that it was designated as a National Historic Landmark in 1985. The Full Scale Tunnel was officially retired from NASA in 1995, and transferred to management by Old Dominion University. It has provided over a decade of contributions to both aerospace and non-aerospace applications.

Activities at the Full Scale Tunnel were rapidly increasing in 1938, and the beginning of World War II would literally jam its test-preparation areas with high-priority test articles. Its unique capabilities were in great demand, particularly for prototype military aircraft. In April 1938, the Brewster XF2A-1 Buffalo fighter was tested in an investigation requested by the Navy to identify modifications to reduce the aerodynamic drag of the airplane. This study precipitated a series of tests of full-scale military aircraft in what became known as drag "clean-up" tests. Over 30 airplanes were ultimately tested for the Army and the Navy during World War II, including three scout bombers, a dive bomber, an attack bomber, a torpedo bomber, a scout observation plane, and 17 fighters. Test shifts extended into round-the-clock operations, including day shifts, night shifts, and "graveyard" shifts.[1]

The XP-39

Jack worked as a research engineer for four and a half years at the Full Scale Tunnel. He participated in stability and control, engine cooling, and drag reduction research that helped win the war. It also shaped the foundation of aeronautical engineering for future generations of designers. The majority of his research involved enhancing the characteristics of the nation's military aircraft during the early years of World War II. During Jack's career at the Full Scale Wind Tunnel, he participated in tests of such well-known aircraft as the Army Curtiss XP-40 and Bell XP-39B fighters, the Navy Curtiss XSOC-1 reconnaissance aircraft, the Navy Grumman XTBF-1 torpedo bomber, the Army Douglas A-20A attack bomber, and a number of unorthodox airplanes, including the V-173 "Flying Flapjack."

Reeder participated in "drag clean-up" studies of the XP-40 in the Full Scale Tunnel in April 1939, as an assistant to established engineers Clint H. Dearborn and Abe Silverstein. These studies were part of a famous contribution of the NACA to improve the top speeds of aircraft through drag reduction. In drag clean-up testing technique, the staff perfected a procedure to isolate the effects of specific airplane components on overall drag. Drag contributed by cracks, crevices and protuberances was measured by first "fairing" the aircraft by covering all cracks and crevices with putty or adhesive tape, then removing the fairings individually to define the impact of specific surface irregularities. Cooling systems were opened, landing gear fairings were uncovered, and canopy fairings were removed to define the individual effects and suggest modifications to reduce drag. The results of the XP-40 studies were summarized in the final NACA Confidential Report, which was co-authored by Dearborn, Silverstein, and Reeder.

The summary was worded in typical fashion for cleanup tests:

> *Based on the test results it is estimated that modifications to the airplane that are immediately practicable such as sealing slots, utilizing trailing antenna, closing spinner holes, fairing landing gear, and modifying the radiator installation would increase the top speed by about 23 miles per hour. Incorporating the further refinements of completely retracting the landing gear, increasing the size of the radiator and providing an optimum radiator duct, smoothing the wing, redesigning the carburetor inlet, redesigning the oil-cooler system so as to obtain a higher duct efficiency, and improving the wing fillets could result in a total increase in maximum speed of about 42 miles per hour.*[2]

Following the clean-up tests, the Army accepted several of the NACA suggestions and the XP-40 was modified. The top speed of the airplane subsequently increased from 330 mph to 360 mph.[3]

In March 1940, Jack served as the lead engineer in charge of Full Scale Tunnel studies requested by the Army Air Corps aimed at improving and refining the aerodynamics of the Bell XP-39B design. The original XP-39 airplane had been the subject of earlier tests in the tunnel in August 1939 under the direction of Silverstein and others.[4] Numerous modifications to the original design were suggested by the NACA staff to the Army, and several of the NACA modifications as well as some originated by the Army were implemented by Bell. Changes made included lowering of the cockpit canopy and full retraction of the landing gear into the wing and fuselage. The Army also demanded the removal of a supercharger that would have enabled the airplane to perform more effectively at higher altitudes. As a result of the lack of a supercharger, the aircraft performed well in combat at lower altitudes, but was not effective at high altitudes. Even today, the lack of a supercharger is cited as a major blunder in the P-39 program.

A-20A Twin Engine Attack Bomber - with outer wing panels removed mounted in the Langley Full Scale Tunnel for engine cooling/aerodynamic performance enhancement testing.

NASA Langley Research Center

After the XP-39 was modified and renamed the XP-39B, flight tests showed performance levels lower than expected and led to the follow-on tests led by Jack with William J. "Bill" Nelson. The range of potential new fixes to the XP-39B to improve performance was severely restricted by the urgency of the tests, which precluded any major structural modifications. Most of the study was directed at the drag induced by the wing-inlet ducts, the carburetor intake, the wheel-well fairing, and defining the benefits of special propeller cuffs that were designed and fabricated by Langley based on positive results obtained during earlier tunnel testing of a XP-39 propeller.[5]

Reeder and Nelson concluded that:

> *The present tunnel tests of this airplane show direct possibilities for increasing the high speed by 18 mph. A further increase of 4 mph will probably be realized by the addition of new propeller cuffs. Further small gains may be made by pinching the exhaust stacks and polishing the propeller blades.*[6]

A-20A Twin Engine Attack Bomber

A-20A twin engine attack bomber with outer wing panels removed mounted in the Langley Full Scale Tunnel for engine cooling/aerodynamic performance enhancement testing.
NASA Langley Research Center

In January 1941, Jack and Herbert A. "Hack" Wilson conducted wind-tunnel studies at the request of the Army to enhance the engine cooling and aerodynamic performance of the Douglas A-20A twin-engine attack bomber. Flight tests of the airplane by the Army and by Douglas had showed that although engine cooling was adequate in cruise flight, the cylinder head temperatures were above the allowable for high-power climb conditions. Douglas had attempted to cure the cooling problem by cutting eight holes in the cowling behind the cylinder baffles, but the high speed of the airplane was lower than desired because of the additional drag. Reeder and Wilson conducted in-depth studies of the nature of the cooling problem and devised new engine cowling installations that could be adapted to later versions of the A-20. The results of their study identified several satisfactory cowling arrangements, including the potential use of blowers and ejector stacks. The suggested modifications contributed to the design of later variants of the A-20, which ultimately became a highly effective ground attack/low-level bomber during the early to middle years of World War II.

General Motors GM A-1 Aerial Torpedo

In August 1941, Jack Reeder led wind-tunnel tests to determine the aerodynamic performance, stability, and control characteristics of the General Motors Aerial Torpedo, an unmanned flying bomb designated as the GM A-1, seen here mounted in the Langley Full Scale Tunnel.

NASA Langley Research Center

In August 1941, at the request of the Army, Jack led wind-tunnel tests to determine the aerodynamic performance, stability, and control characteristics of the General Motors Aerial Torpedo, an unmanned flying bomb known as the GM A-1. In September 1939, unmanned aviation pioneer Charles F. Kettering of General Motors had proposed a radio-controlled flying bomb to the Army Air Corps. Kettering had received widespread notoriety for his invention of the Kettering "Bug", an unmanned flying bomb fabricated in 1918 during the last years of World War I. The Army had ordered about 50 Bugs, but it was never used in combat. The Bug was launched from a track, from which it would fly along a straight path toward enemy lines. A counter would keep track of the number of revolutions made by the propeller, and at the desired time, fuel to the engine would be cut off, a cam fell into place to fold the wings, and the Bug would plunge to earth and explode. The Bug had no direct control. An altitude sensor and pneumatic controls based on bellows from a player piano controlled its climb.[7]

A 200 hp piston engine powered the GM A-1. It was launched from a four-wheeled dolly, and was designed to carry a 500 lb. bomb over a distance of 400 miles. The unmanned drone had elevator and rudder controls automatically operated by an altimeter and a directional gyro. It was catapulted at a speed of 100 miles per hour, after which it rose to a preset altitude and flew at 200 miles per hour along a preset course. The airplane had a span of approximately 21 feet and weighed 1250 pounds, fully loaded. The Army had ordered ten prototypes in 1941, and a wind-tunnel assessment of the airplane in the Full Scale Tunnel was requested.

Reeder and fellow engineer G. Merritt Preston ran exhaustive tests to determine the control positions required to trim the airplane, and included powered tests to determine the effects of propeller slipstream. Stability was measured about all three axes and flying characteristics were projected. In their report to the Army, they reported that "The static stability and control effectiveness of the airplane were found to be ample and that the top speed of the drone would be about 198 miles per hour based on the tunnel data."[8] The results of the tunnel tests indicated no "show stoppers" for the design, but a series of crashes associated with its launch and guidance systems led to cancellation of the project in 1943.

The Vought-Sikorsky V-173 "Flying Pancake"

The Vought-Sikorsky V-173 in flight.

Larry Loftin

One of the most unconventional aircraft designs tested by Jack was the Vought-Sikorsky V-173 "Flying Pancake" in November 1941. This aerial anomaly was designed by Charles H. Zimmerman, one of the most innovative aeronautical engineers to ever work at the LMAL. Zimmerman was an expert in applied aerodynamics and flight dynamics. He designed and oversaw the development of the NACA Langley Spin Tunnel and Free-Flight Tunnel, and he was the inventor of the Hiller "Flying Platform" tested by the Army in the 1950's. Zimmerman pursued the "Pancake" shape as a concept to provide Short Take-Off and Landing (STOL) capability. With its low-aspect-ratio, almost circular wing and large counter-rotating propellers, experts projected the possibility of extremely low approach and landing speeds. Zimmerman had matured his unconventional concept with small-scale model studies from 1933 to 1937 as a Langley engineer. With the approval of the NACA, Zimmerman approached United Aircraft Corporation with his novel design in 1937 and joined United's Chance Vought Aircraft Division in that year as a project engineer. The V-173 was intended to be a flight-worthy experimental aircraft to demonstrate the pancake-wing concept and to serve as a precursor to advanced military versions.

The V-173 tunnel tests in the Full Scale Tunnel were conducted at the request of the Navy's Bureau of Aeronautics to assess the aerodynamic performance, drag characteristics, and airflow phenomena associated with the design (especially propeller slipstream effects). At the time of the tests, the relatively lightweight V-173 was to be flown with two 75-horsepower engines; however, a high-speed military version of the concept was to be powered by two 2000-horsepower engines. The tunnel tests were intended to provide data that might be useful in the design of the higher-powered airplane (ultimately to be known as the XF5U-1).

Jack Reeder's leadership in the tests extended beyond obtaining conventional data from the tunnel scale system, to personally measuring control characteristics. Jack said "I sat in the cockpit while the plane was mounted in the wind tunnel measuring forces using hand-held springs."[10] His measurements of aerodynamic data also included extensive pressure distributions for power-on and power-off conditions.

Reeder and his associate, Gerald W. "Jerry" Brewer, conducted exhaustive testing and defined the aerodynamic characteristics of the V-173 in detail. In their memorandum report for the Navy, they made several conclusions focused on the aerodynamic effects of the large propellers. They concluded that: "(1) the inherently high induced drag of a low-aspect-ratio circular wing can be partially compensated by the favorable interaction of large-diameter propellers operating ahead of the wing; (2) the effects of the operation of large-diameter propellers ahead of a wing are equivalent to an increase in the wing span since it results in increasing the mass of air to which downward momentum is imparted by the lifting force; (3) the reduction in the induced drag and increased propulsive efficiency obtained with propeller operation is dependent only in a minor way on the relative direction of the rotation of the propeller and the tip vortices; (4) propeller operation on the V-173 airplane arrangement affects a large decrease in the longitudinal stability due to the lift on the propellers and the slipstream rotation at the tail; and (5) rotation of the propellers opposite to the present arrangement so that they turn in the same direction as the tip vortices would result in greatly increased stability with only slight decreases in the propulsive efficiency."[11]

The V-173, intended for use as a STOL flight demonstrator, was initially flown on November 23, 1942. The aircraft performed surprisingly well in flight, and in 1941 Chance Vought received a Navy contract to further develop the design, under the designation XF5U-1. Tests of a large-scale model of the XF5U-1 were conducted in the Full Scale Tunnel at the request of the Navy in mid-1945. The Navy seriously considered using the XF5U-1, with its excellent short-takeoff-and-landing and high-speed characteristics, as an interceptor against Japanese Kamikaze aircraft that posed a serious threat to U.S. naval warships in the Pacific during the latter stages of World War II. However, the war ended before the aircraft could be pressed into service and the emergence of the jet fighter caused the Navy to lose interest in the XF5U-1 program. Although the program was cancelled and the aircraft never flew, it did contribute useful design data for postwar V/STOL aircraft designs. The V-173 presently is part of the aeronautical collection of the National Air and Space Museum of the Smithsonian Institution.

Navy Grumman XTBF-1 Torpedo Bomber

Jack's wind-tunnel testing career continued at a blistering pace. In the summer of 1942, he led drag clean-up studies of the Grumman XTBF-1, prototype of the famous Navy Avenger torpedo bomber. The XTBF-1 drag clean-up studies were some of the most rigorous aerodynamic efforts conducted by the staff of the Full Scale Tunnel and serve today as textbook examples of drag-reduction technology, much of which is applicable to propeller-driven general aviation aircraft. Together with his associate engineer, William J. Biebel, Jack went through a systematic study that began with drag measurements with the airplane completely faired and sealed, and continued in successive stages until the airplane was returned to its service condition. Control effectiveness was measured in power-on and off conditions, cooling-air pressures were measured, pressure distributions were measured on the canopy and turret to determine air loads, and the effects of wing-mounted radar installations were evaluated. Their final report to the Navy's Bureau of Aeronautics was a treasure of unprecedented data on the effects of aircraft components and physical condition on drag.[12]

In the summer of 1942, Jack led drag clean-up studies of the Navy Grumman XTBF-1 Avenger torpedo bomber.

NASA Langley Research Center

Reeder authored or coauthored a total of nine technical reports that "was quite a respectable output for the four and one half years he spent as a member of the staff of the Full Scale Tunnel."[13] Jack was rapidly able to apply his university training in aeronautical engineering and hone his skills in aerodynamics. Most importantly, he associated with and assisted some of the most outstanding practical engineers in the NACA. Many of these professionals became future leaders within the NACA and were internationally recognized for their expertise. "One of his daily contacts was Abe Silverstein, a renowned authority in aerodynamics, who later became Director of the NASA Lewis Research Center, and another of his daily contacts was Harry J. Goett, who later served as a senior Division Chief at the Ames Research Center and was then appointed as the first

Director of the NASA Goddard Space Flight Center."[14] Reeder's passion for flying did not diminish during his wind-tunnel activities at the Full-Scale Tunnel.

Private Pilot License Training

In August 1939, Jack earned his private pilots license. As part of the requirements for his pilots license, he accumulated a total of 35 hours of flying time in a Piper J-3 Cub similar to the one depicted here.

Larry Loftin

In the Fall of 1938, he took on the task of becoming a student pilot in his spare time. He learned how to fly conventional aircraft at a tiny "airport", consisting of two grass covered airstrips, at nearby Newport News, Virginia. The location was known as Morgan's Field. "The cost of $3.00 per hour included rental of the aircraft as well as an instructor's 'fee', a modest amount of money even for that era."[15] Jack eventually soloed following eight hours of instruction and was awarded his private pilots license in August 1939. He accumulated a total of 35 hours of flying time in a Piper J-3 Cub, successfully meeting the requirement. "As an indication of the level of proficiency required to obtain a private pilots license at that time, absolutely no instruction was given in cross-wind operations. Stalling speed of the Cub was sufficiently low so that landings and takeoffs could be made directly into the wind, either along or across the runway as prevailing conditions might dictate. Furthermore, there was no ground school of any kind. Knowledge of navigation or meteorology, for example, had to be acquired by self-study undertaken on the student's own initiative."[16]

Jack Reeder performing maintenance on his 1930 Model 90 Monocoupe.

Jack Reeder

Following acceptance of his pilot's license, Reeder and a fellow engineer from Langley bought a 1930 model 90 Monocoupe. "The airplane was powered by a 90 hp, 5-cylinder Lambert radial engine. Except for a few collectors of antique and historic aircraft, the Monocoupe is virtually unknown today; in the time period between its first flight in 1927 and World War II, however, it was extremely popular. Such aviation notables as Charles Lindbergh, Anthony Fokker, John Livingston, and Jack Wright flew the type. In addition to routine use by private pilots, modified versions of the aircraft were profitably employed for racing and aerobatics. The Monocoupe was a trim, high-wing monoplane with side-by-side seating for two people in a small enclosed cabin. Gross weight of the model 90 version was 1585 pounds, and maximum speed was between 115 and 120 mph depending upon the engine."[17]

Jack thoroughly enjoyed flying his Monocoupe, but one day became involved in his first crash. He later recalled:

> *In comparison with the Cub, the Monocoupe was of relatively high performance and had a wing loading nearly twice that of the little trainer. Because of the higher landing speed of the Monocoupe, landing across the runway was no longer feasible and cross-wind landings were sometimes necessary. Also, the aircraft was cleaner than the Cub and did not decelerate nearly as rapidly from normal approach speeds. On one particular day, I had to land with a strong cross-wind over the grass runway. Without prior training in cross-wind landing techniques, I tried ruddering (or kicking-out) the drift angle, wings level, just prior to expected touchdown on the wheels. However, I did not touchdown but floated and 'kicked' several times in the same direction until touchdown finally occurred in the three-point attitude. I then found myself facing a ditch at the edge of the runway and opened the throttle all the way. I jumped the ditch but stalled at a height of about three feet. The aircraft hit on the wheels and flipped tail over nose as it rebounded, with the vertical tail being the first to hit the ground as the aircraft came to rest in the inverted position. The tail and aft fuselage were badly damaged, but the wing hit the ground in a flat attitude and only three ribs were broken. The safety belt was, of course, a life saver. However, despite my best efforts to support myself with one arm, I fell mighty hard on my head when I released the belt with my other hand, which was an eventuality I had not considered beforehand. As a result of this accident, I became determined to master successful crosswind landing techniques."[18]*

The aircraft was eventually repaired and flown numerous times before being sold to Republic employee Jim Roye in Long Island. During the early 1980's, Reeder became the proud owner of a vintage 1937 Monocoupe.

In his quest to discover the flight performance and flying qualities of additional airplane designs, Reeder flew other light aircraft, including a Waco biplane that featured three seats and an open cockpit. The airplane used a 5-cylinder Kinner radial engine capable of 125 hp. Jack summarized his experience with this airplane:

> *It was a new and exciting experience to sit in the open, noisy, drafty cockpit with helmet and goggles and look above and behind the airplane without restriction. However, the goggles gave the impression of wearing a pair of horse blinders. I remember particularly looking back over the tail, seeing the controls move, and watching the runway recede in the distance in similar fashion to the flying scenes from the movies about World War I. The tail wheel of this airplane swiveled but was not steerable. Braking was applied by pulling the throttle handle to the left, which was pivoted at its base, and steering with the rudder pedals to control the braking differentially. One day, I was taxiing the length of the runway to take-off position with a light tailwind. It suddenly occurred to me that I might be taxiing too fast to avert a ground loop should the airplane start to swerve. I closed the throttle to idle and a swerve began almost immediately. I applied opposite rudder and increased braking to no avail, and the turn rate increased to a point where the braking accelerated the turn. I looked with alarm and despair at the outside lower wingtip that was dragging on the ground. The wingtip was deflected upward and the fabric covering was badly wrinkled. Typically, the ground loop stopped after about 270 degrees of turn with the aircraft rolling backward in its stable configuration (center of gravity now ahead of the main wheels). I had experienced my first ground loop! Fortunately, we found that the damage was limited to a single broken rib.[19]*

The Ercoupe

Designed by famous Langley engineer Fred E. Weick. Weick who also invented the NACA radial engine cowling that was applied to radial engine propeller-driven aircraft throughout the world and the tricycle landing gear configuration for aircraft.

Larry Loftin

Another airplane Reeder enjoyed flying was the Ercoupe, designed by famous Langley engineer Fred E. Weick, who had led Langley's efforts in the development of the famous NACA radial engine cowling concept which became a standard feature on aircraft all over the world, and the tricycle landing gear configuration (as initially applied to his home-built experimental W-1 aircraft).

The Ercoupe configuration featured a low-mounted wing with a then unusual tricycle landing gear and twin vertical tails. Nose-wheel steering was provided through the flight control wheel that also actuated the ailerons and added coordinating rudder for airborne turns. Thus, the Ercoupe was a two-control airplane in the sense that no rudder pedals were provided for the pilot. It was claimed that the aircraft would not spin and could not be stalled in unaccelerated flight. Two people were seated side-by-side in an enclosed cockpit. Power was supplied by a 4-cylinder, horizontally opposed, air-cooled engine of 65 hp account of the problems he encountered in landing the Ercoupe in a crosswind follows:

On the day of my flight, there was a strong cross-wind at about 45 degrees to both of the grass runways. The airplane was intended to be landed while crabbing into the crosswind with wings level, as otherwise, with the two-control arrangement, a turn would result. After landing, the nose was to be lowered to the ground and the control wheel immediately released to allow the nose wheel and subsequently the aircraft to align with the direction of motion over the ground. On my first landing with a large crab angle, I lowered the nose wheel and turned the controls loose somewhat late. Instead of straightening to align with the runway, the aircraft turned 90 degrees to the ground track, then shuddered and jumped sideways to a halt in a most alarming fashion. Although I quickly turned the control wheel loose on my second landing, the same thing happened again. My friend who owned the airplane had not experienced this behavior, so he tried another landing on the other runway. The same sequence of maneuvers resulted. The aircraft remained laterally level on its landing gear in all of these cases. Apparently the sidewise sliding friction on the main gear when on grass was less than the restraint on the nose wheel and the aircraft performed a 90-degree ground loop. Thus, one drawback to this particular two-control arrangement was revealed. Of course the aircraft did not behave this way on a paved surface.[20]

While Jack was pursuing his career and personal interests in the Tidewater area of Virginia, his love life was beginning to take off as well. Frances Winder first met Jack Reeder in 1938 at NACA Langley when he arrived there after graduating from the University of Michigan. Frances worked at Langley as a stenographer, and she worked for famous Langley Directors, including Henry J. E. Reid. Frances recalled "At that time, the NACA was a small, sociable group. Everybody knew everyone else. So it was inevitable that we would meet at a party or a dance. It was sort of questionable which one it was, and it wasn't love at first sight. Although I thought he was a great dancer, and I liked the way he danced. I remembered him from the very first time I met him at a dance. Anyhow we just met as mutual friends."[21] A courtship that lasted 6 years ensued until the couple decided to marry early in 1944. They were married in Hampton on January 26, 1944.

Upon America's entry into World War II, general aviation (GA) flights by civilians were prohibited in the U.S., which forced Jack and his engineer friend to sell their 1930 model 90 Monocoupe. By then, Reeder had accumulated a total of 168 hours of flight time in nine GA aircraft. While his flying pursuits appeared to be over, a stroke of good fortune occurred in October 1942. By that time, Langley's surplus of quality research pilots was being drained by the establishment of two additional NACA Laboratories – the NACA Aircraft Engine Research Laboratory (which later became known as the Lewis Flight Propulsion Laboratory) in Cleveland, Ohio, and the NACA Ames Aeronautical Laboratory in Mountain View, California at Moffet Field.

Melvin Gough

NACA's first Engineering Test Pilot and Head of NACA Flight Operations at Langley when Jack sought to transfer to the NACA's Flight Operations Division. Gough later served as Jack's boss for several years before moving on to a position of leadership at NASA's Cape Canaveral Station (now Kennedy Space Center) in Florida with the advent of the Space Program.

NASA Langley Research Center via Larry Loftin

Melvin Gough, the first NACA Engineering Test Pilot who came to Langley in 1926 and later became Head of NACA Flight Operations at Langley, received a directive from his superiors at NACA Headquarters in Washington, D.C. to choose and groom qualified volunteers for flight research duty among the engineers at Langley.

NACA Ryan ST trainer at Langley.

NASA Langley Research Center via Larry Loftin

Needless to say, Jack was eager to serve and became one of the first volunteers to apply for a position. "Reeder later recalled his initial meeting with Gough as being in two parts. First, there was a verbal interview that lasted for perhaps an hour. After the interview, he was taken for a flight in a NACA Ryan ST that was a relatively high performance, open cockpit, low-wing monoplane.

Jack rode in the front cockpit. Gough put the aircraft into inverted flight that resulted in Jack receiving a spray of gasoline in the face; apparently, the flight was to determine if the applicant would panic or perhaps become sick from the gasoline in inverted flight. Jack did neither."[22]

This convinced Gough and others in the Flight Operations Division that he was fit for duty. He was selected for official flight research duty in Summer 1942, but did not start as a flight research pilot until October 1942 because he had to complete his written technical report on his Vought V-173 wind-tunnel studies. However, he was now an engineering test pilot in the Flight Research Division at Langley. Finally, a dream had become reality and another segment of his remarkable career was about to take flight.

Portrait of Jack Reeder at the time of his transfer to the NACA Langley Flight Operations Division in October 1942.

NASA Langley Research Center via Larry Loftin

Chapter 2 Notes

1. Gray, George W. (1948). <u>Frontiers of Flight</u>. Alfred A. Knopf, New York.

2. Dearborn, C. H.; Silverstein, Abe; and Reeder, J. P. (May 16, 1939). <u>Army Air Corps Material Division, War Department Test of XP-40 Airplane in NACA Full-Scale Tunnel</u>. National Advisory Committee for Aeronautics, Langley Memorial Aeronautical Laboratory, Langley Field, Va., p. 17.

3. Gray, George W. (1948). <u>Frontiers of Flight</u>. Alfred A. Knopf, New York.

4. Silverstein, Abe, and Nickle, F.R. (September 27, 1939). <u>Tests of the XP-39 Airplane in the N.A.C.A. Full-Scale Wind Tunnel</u>. Confidential Report for the Army Air Corps, Material Division, War Department, N.A.C.A.

5. McHugh, James G. (1939). <u>Tests of XP-39 Airplane Propeller with and without Shank Fairings</u>. Confidential Memorandum for Army Air Corps, Materials Division, NACA.

6. Reeder, John P. and Nelson, William J. (March 16, 1940). <u>Army Air Corps, Materiel Division, War Department Tests of the XP-39B Airplane in the NACA Full-Scale Wind Tunnel</u>. National Advisory Committee for Aeronautics, Langley Memorial Aeronautical Laboratory, Langley Field, Va., pp. 10-11.

7. DeGaspari, John (2003). "Look Ma, No Pilot!". Mechanical Engineering Magazine of The American Society of Mechanical Engineers.

8. Reeder, John P. and Preston, G. Merritt (October 29, 1941). <u>Memorandum Report for the Army Air Corps Full-Scale Wind Tunnel Tests of the General Motors Aerial Torpedo</u>. National Advisory Committee for Aeronautics, Langley Memorial Aeronautical Laboratory, Langley Field, Va., pp. 1, 8.

9. Werrell, Kenneth P. (1985). <u>The Evolution of the Cruise Missile</u>. Air University Press.

10. Interview with John P. Reeder (March 21, 1994). Newport News, Va.

11. Reeder, John P. and Brewer, Gerald W. (April 28, 1941). <u>Memorandum Report for Bureau of Aeronautics, Navy Department, NACA Full-Scale Wind-Tunnel Tests of Vought Sikorsky V-173 Airplane</u>. National Advisory Committee for Aeronautics, Langley Memorial Aeronautical Laboratory, Langley Field, Va., pp. 23-24.

12. Reeder, John P. and Biebel, William J. (October 21, 1942). <u>Memorandum Report for Bureau of Aeronautics, Navy Department, Tests of Grumman XTBF-1 Airplane in the NACA Full-Scale Tunnel</u>. National Advisory Committee for Aeronautics, Langley Memorial Aeronautical Laboratory, Langley Field, Va., pp. 16-17.

13. Loftin, Laurence K., Jr. (Unpublished Manuscript, July 1986). <u>A Research Pilot's World As Seen From The Cockpit Of A NASA Engineer-Pilot</u>, Chap. 2, p. 9.

14. Ibid.

15. Ibid., Chap. 2, p. 10.

16. Ibid.

17. Ibid., Chap. 2, p. 12.

18. Ibid., Chap. 2, p. 13.

19. Ibid., Chap. 2, p. 15.

20. Ibid., Chap. 2, p. 16.

21. Interview with Mrs. Frances Winder Reeder and Shirley Reeder Randall (March 20, 2006). Newport News, Va.

22. Loftin, Laurence K., Jr. (Unpublished Manuscript, July 1986). <u>A Research Pilot's World As Seen From The Cockpit Of A NASA Engineer-Pilot</u>, Chap. 3, p. 11.

Chapter Three
A Career Takes Flight

NACA flight research pilots at the LMAL in December 1944.

From left to right top row: Stefan Cavallo, William Gray Jr., Jack Reeder; From left to right bottom row: Melvin Gough, William McAvoy, and Herbert Hoover.

NASA Langley Research Center via Larry Loftin

Jack Reeder's intense passion for flying emerged with all its energy upon his transfer to Langley's flight research organization. Jack's perspectives on the daily life of research pilots and his expectations of the challenges of his new career demanded a clear understanding of the unique characteristics and demands of a research test pilot. Even today, many do not appreciate the differences between their perceptions and the reality of a test pilot's life. Before discussing Jack's activities as a NACA pilot, it is appropriate to more fully define the research pilot and his tasks. With this background, the reader can better appreciate the environment that Reeder encountered and conquered.

Jack's friend, Larry Loftin, had a strong concern over the misconceptions held by most of the public regarding test pilots, and he was frequently outspoken on the subject:

> *In the public eye, test pilots are usually perceived as dashing, glamorous and utterly fearless young knights of the air. They put new and untried aircraft into screaming power dives followed by high-g pull-outs to determine whether the wings and other parts of the aircraft will remain in one piece, or whether the entire machine will disintegrate and kill the leather-clad hero, or perhaps allow him to return safely to earth hanging beneath his faithful parachute. Much of his lurid and highly exaggerated image is pure myth and may result, at least in part, from the action packed motion pictures of the 1930's and 1940's, many of which appear with regularity on late television shows.*
>
> *In the 1920s and 1930s, the test pilot community – including pilots within the NACA – was characterized by activities consisting of a combination of test flying together with air racing and various other types of spectacular aviation activities. Generally, these daredevil gypsy pilots had no engineering education and flew strictly by the seat of their pants without regard to quantitative scientific measurements. Their impact on future aeronautical development, though requiring considerable piloting skill and personal courage, was not nearly so great as that of other test pilots engaged in less spectacular but more quantitative and analytical types of experimental flying. This type of precise*

> *test flying with highly instrumented aircraft has always provided an important and productive link between the world of the cockpit and the theoretical, design and engineering aspects of the science of aeronautics. Actually, although methods and test techniques have changed and become vastly more specialized and sophisticated with the passage of time, engineering test flying is as old as flying itself. Surely, the Wright Brothers were among the first of the great aeronautical engineers and test pilots.[1]*

Loftin also pointed out the basic differences between "contemporary" test pilots and "experimental" test pilots, which still apply today:

> *Contemporary test flying covers a wide range of diverse activities which require a variety of skills and results in the development of many different specialists. Broadly speaking, however, modern test pilots fall into one of two distinctly different categories: namely, production test pilots and experimental test pilots. The duties of a production test pilot require that he test fly each new aircraft of a given type as it rolls off the production line. These aircraft are of specified design and incorporate no significant engineering departures from that design. Flight tests are made of each new aircraft to ensure that all systems function in the required manner, and that the aircraft meets certain specified performance characteristics. Put another way, these flight tests are made to demonstrate that the aircraft has been manufactured according to contract requirements and meets all contract specifications…*

> *In contrast to many production test pilots, present-day experimental test pilots are usually trained aeronautical engineers, and many have attended one of the test pilot schools operated by the military services; Edwards Air Force Base in the Mojave Desert of California is the home of the USAF test pilot school, and the Patuxent River Naval Air Station in Southern Maryland plays host to the Navy Test Pilot School. Precise and repeatable piloting techniques and special flight maneuvers as well as methods of analyzing flight test data in engineering terms form important parts of the curricula of these schools…*

> *Because of the diverse activities of experimental test pilots, a single definition describing such an individual is extremely difficult and perhaps impossible to formulate. Generally, however, the experimental test pilot may be described as one who flies aircraft in an organized technical program with a view toward providing quantitative data, along with expert pilot opinion and recommendations, related to some important area of flight…*

> *Every major aircraft manufacturer employs a staff of engineering test pilots. When the development of a new aircraft is begun, a project pilot is usually assigned early in*

the design process. His comments and recommendations play an important part in the development of the aircraft, particularly in regard to stability, control and handling characteristics throughout the flight envelope, flight safety, and in the design and layout of the flight deck. The test pilot usually makes extensive simulator studies of the flight behavior of the new aircraft, so that by the time of the first flight, he has considerable confidence in his understanding of the flying characteristics to be expected. Yet, surprises can and do occur, and the pilot's comments and recommendations play an important part in ensuring that the correct aircraft modifications are incorporated in the design.

Several years may be required to test completely a new aircraft following first flight. All aspects of the behavior of aircraft must be explored and documented by the project pilot and his associates working with the project engineering staff. Satisfaction of the Federal Aviation Administration (FAA) authorities as to the airworthiness of the new aircraft, and the customer as to the performance guarantees and other significant characteristics, are required in the development and sale of a new commercial aircraft. FAA and customer pilots and engineers must be satisfied. In a new military aircraft, service pilots and engineers participate in the selection (or rejection) of a new aircraft. Certainly, the job of the experimental test pilot is an important and demanding one. The scope of these activities is broad and varies according to the particular circumstance of his position.

Research pilots, a special class of experimental test pilot, frequently fall into the category of those pilots who are masters of most or all of the important specialty areas. Such pilots are usually devoted solely to the advancement of the technology of flight and, with certain exceptions usually engendered by some sort of national or industry wide emergency, are not concerned with the detailed development of a particular vehicle. Research pilots are, for the most part, employed by some agency of the federal government or by a private research organization. The research pilots found on the staffs of the research centers of the National Aeronautics and Space Administration (NASA) and its predecessor organization, the National Advisory Committee for Aeronautics (NACA), have long been held in his esteem by all elements of the aeronautical community.[2]

The Curtiss JN-4H Jennies

In June 1919, the NACA began its first flight research studies at the LMAL with two Curtiss JN-4H Jennies procured from the US Army Air Service. The planes were piloted by Thomas Carroll and Edmund

The first of two Curtiss JN-4H Jennies procured by the NACA from the US Army Air Service being prepared for flight research studies at LMAL in June 1919. At the controls in the aircraft were Thomas Carroll and Edmund T. "Eddie" Allen, the agency's first two test pilots who had no formal education in aeronautical engineering.

NASA Langley Research Center via National Archives at College Park, Maryland

The NACA's first flight research missions involved the correlation of flight data with data generated from wind-tunnel studies of Jenny models. Here, an NACA Jenny test pilot had deployed a pitot-static tube to record the aircraft's airspeed.

NASA Langley Research Center

A lineup of flight research subjects on the NACA side of Langley Field in 1944. The lineup was indicative of the amount of ongoing flight research projects at the LMAL during World War II.

NASA Langley Research Center

T. "Eddie" Allen, the agency's first two test pilots. Their first mission involved the correlation of flight data with data generated from wind-tunnel studies of Jenny models.

The formal NACA technical report generated from this first flight test recommended that a special research pilot, one with extensive experience in the field of aeronautical engineering, be sought for future flight research purposes. Thus, the term "Engineering Pilot" was created and designated to those performing flight research for the NACA and later NASA. Over the years, NACA/NASA Langley employed several pilots that fit this mold, but none has fit the description better than Jack Reeder..

In order to qualify for flying high-performance piston engine military aircraft, research pilots at Langley had to follow a specific pilot training regimen or routine. This procedure involved mastering flight in different types of aircraft according to level of sophistication, gradually working up the chain until mastery of flight in the most sophisticated aircraft was achieved. "As the pilot trainee progressed, he flew aircraft of increasing weight, power, wing loading (weight per square foot of wing area), and reduced power loading (engine horsepower per square foot of wing area).

Test pilot Jack Reeder boarding a Curtiss P-40F Warhawk prior to performing an evaluation flight at Langley in October 1943.

NASA Langley Research Center via Larry Loftin

Thus, the student was required to fly and demonstrate proficiency in aircraft of increased power and performance as he progressed through the course. Initial training was provided by a group of increasingly sophisticated general aviation types: the Piper Cub, Fairchild XR2K-1 (civil model 22), Ryan ST, and Stinson SR8E; after which came the Navy advanced trainer, the North American SNJ (similar to the Army AT-6), followed by a succession of single engine fighters, dive bombers, a torpedo bomber, and a twin engine aircraft, the Lockheed 12. Student research pilots also received other types of training in addition to flying the various types of aircraft. Attendance at pre- and post-flight briefings with project engineers and pilots provided useful insights into the techniques of research piloting, methods of measuring and recording data, and the close working relationships between pilots and engineers. Special night classes sponsored by Langley in cooperation with the University of Virginia were also available. One especially valuable course dealt with the measurement and evaluation of aircraft handling qualities.

The instructor was Langley's Robert R. Gilruth, who earlier had developed and published the first comprehensive set of requirements for satisfactory flying qualities for aircraft."[3]

As 1943 drew to a close, Reeder had successfully completed flights in a total of 19 aircraft. "Nine of these happened to be single-seat fighters and his total number of hours flown during the year was about 323. Additional time of about 11 hours and 15 hours were spent under the hood in flight and in the Link Trainer (the Link Trainer was an early ground-based simulator with limited motion which was used for learning and practicing instrument flying techniques and procedures), respectively."[4]

Jack's first flight research task involved flying the Brewster XSBA-1 scout bomber in a series of stability and control studies at the request of the Navy. As a result of the flight evaluation performed by Reeder, design modifications – in particular adjusting the dihedral angle of the wings – were subsequently made to the airplane that improved its handling qualities. At the time, this kind of research could only be performed through flight tests in which the aircraft was flown with the wings manually adjusted at varying angles between the flight tests. With the advent of sophisticated computer technology and simulators, engineers can presently study such modifications on aircraft on the ground.

A Harrowing Episode

Vought F4U-1 "Birdcage" Corsair parked on runway following Jack Reeder's harrowing test flight in which oil leaked from the engine, coating the aircraft with an extensive slick. Note the oil slick covering the fuselage and part of the right wing of the aircraft.

NASA Langley Research Center

Close up view of engine cowling and forward fuselage of Vought F4U-1 Birdcage Corsair following Jack Reeder's test flight in which engine oil coated the aircraft with an extensive slick.

NASA Langley Research Center

The first fighter evaluated by Reeder was the Army Curtiss XP-42, derived from the Pre-World War II Curtiss P-36 Hawk design. The XP-42 featured a new engine cowling perfected by the NACA, as well as an innovative all-moving horizontal stabilizer for enhanced maneuverability. However, not all of Reeder's flights went well in 1943. He later recalled a rather harrowing episode:

> In 1943, I had my first real emergency after transferring to the NACA piloting staff. I was flying an F4U-1 Corsair, one of the early versions which had the low cockpit and seat, the 'birdcage' canopy and the low tailwheel. Also, the cowl-flap opening extended over the top of the fuselage ahead of the canopy. A hydraulic torquemeter, using engine oil, was installed for power measurements. Suddenly, while flying northwest of Newport News at about 4000 feet, a torquemeter pressure line on the engine face, carrying oil at 400 psi, broke. A thick blanket of oil rolled over the windshield and airplane. I had to open the canopy to see outside. The cockpit and I were soon bathed with oil, and I had to raise my goggles to see at all. I decided everything was too slippery to bail out safely, so I headed for Langley to land.
>
> Observers thought I was on fire. As I leaned to the left edge of the cockpit to see a little better for the approach, flying oil and the windblast made it difficult to determine my orientation. I tried to wipe and pull down my goggles again but the wind took them away.
>
> The last time I saw the runway was on the base leg. I had to prejudge the turn into final and the proper descent path, while keeping my head well inside the edge of the windshield to prevent my left eye from being closed by the wind. As I approached the threshold, I judged height and flare distance by the tails of B-24's on the adjacent taxiway waiting for takeoff. Touchdown was on the runway, wheels first with tail slightly low and with a slight impact. The airplane began to bounce (the very reason the F4U-1 did not qualify for carrier operation originally). The lower I pushed the nose, the more severe the bounce. I then discovered that I had left the throttle cracked and the bouncing stopped as soon as I closed the throttle fully. I stopped on the runway, but getting down from the high cockpit, using all the little steps provided, was hazardous because of the total oil slick. I realized I had not become nervous or upset —too busy!²

As a result of his experience with the Corsair, Reeder's suggestions for improving the aircraft design, replacing the original tail wheel configuration with a raised tail wheel configuration, and raising the cockpit for enhanced visibility were implemented in the production version. This modification helped the aircraft to become an exceptional fighter.

Jack was also involved in a rather humorous incident that occurred while test flying the early version of the Corsair. As recalled by a former NASA Langley engineer who knew Jack, "I remember Jack Reeder talking about flight testing the F4U Corsair. One day, he was working through the flight card on a test flight and he thought he would test the relief tube. As he tested the tube, it blew back at him and he emphatically noted on the flight card: 'Change location of relief tube exit.'"[6]

The P-47D Thunderbolt

In 1943, Reeder also had the opportunity to evaluate two remarkable fighters that ultimately turned the tide of the air war in Europe: the Republic P-47 Thunderbolt and North American P-51 Mustang. Reeder flew several versions of the Thunderbolt and Mustang, including the P-47C, P-47D, XP-51, P-51B, P-51D, and P-51H in flight handling and performance studies.

One of the last versions of the Thunderbolt produced, the P-47D-30, which saw combat in Europe in early 1945 was flight evaluated by Reeder and the airplane's flight characteristics described in detail in the following excerpt from an official NACA Technical Note:

> *Flight tests have been made to determine the longitudinal stability and control and stalling characteristics of an F-47D-30 airplane. The results of these tests show the airplane to be unstable with stick free in any power-on condition even at the most forward center-of-gravity position tested. At the rearward center-of-gravity position tested the airplane also had neutral to negative stick-fixed stability with power on. The characteristics in accelerated flight were acceptable at the forward center-of-gravity position at low and high altitudes except at high speed where the control-force variations with acceleration were high. At the rearward center-of-gravity position, elevator-force reversals were experienced in turns at low speeds, and the elevator-force variations with acceleration were low at all the other speeds tested. Ample stall warning was afforded in all the conditions tested and the stalling characteristics were satisfactory except in the approach and wave-off conditions.*[7]

One of the American fighter workhorses of the European Air War was the P-47D Thunderbolt. Here, Jack Reeder can be seen putting a P-47D-30 through the paces. Note the propeller wake survey rakes on the forward fuselage of the aircraft used to measure propeller thrust and wake. The NACA also conducted flight experiments with the airplane using various propeller blade configurations. This particular aircraft has three propeller blades instead of the normal four blades found on most Thunderbolts during the war.

NASA Langley Research Center via Jack Reeder

The XP-51 Mustang

Jack's all-time favorite WWII fighter was undoubtedly the Mustang. The aircraft set a precedent in its time because it utilized the revolutionary NACA laminar flow airfoil, one of the key factors that enabled it to be such an effective fighter. According to Jack, the airplane "was a 'very fine flying machine' and one of the best fighters he had ever flown."[8] He particularly admired the XP-51 Mustang prototype. Reeder also later added that "when the XP-51 came out it could fly 30 mph faster than any comparable fighter plane of its time."[9] Reeder was chosen to fly flight evaluations of the XP-51 following modifications that had been made to the aileron systems based on recommendations by the NACA. These modifications proved to be significant improvements in the airplane's control and maneuverability. Jack flew the fourth XP-51 (serial number 41-38) in 1944 and was very impressed by its stability and controllability. That particular XP-51 aircraft is presently part of the collection of the AirVenture Museum of Experimental Aircraft Association at Oshkosh, Wisconsin.

Jack Reeder performing a flight evaluation of the North American P-51H Mustang, one of the last versions of the Mustang to be produced. The late-war versions of the Mustang, P-47 Thunderbolt, and Grumman F8F Bearcat featured bubble-top canopies that greatly enhanced the pilot's vision. The H-model Mustang also featured a taller vertical tail for improved stability and control.

(NASA Langley Research Center via Jack Reeder)

Immediately following World War II, Jack Reeder performed flight tests in P-51D Mustangs equipped with special wing test sections with various aircraft model wing and fuselage halves mounted on them for transonic wing flow tests. This Mustang has a delta wing model mounted on its wing. The P-51D was put into a steep dive by the pilot and as the aircraft approached transonic speeds data regarding air flow over the wing model designs mounted on the Mustang's wing was recorded. This test method was conceived by Langley's Dr. Robert Gilruth.

NASA Langley Research Center via Larry Loftin

An advanced swept wing jet model mounted and flight tested on a P-51D.

NASA Langley Research Center via Larry Loftin

Mark Chambers

One of the last versions of the Mustang produced, the P-51H became the subject of extensive study by the NACA. Jack served as the lead test pilot for this study. As stated in the NACA Research Memorandum for the Air Force:

> *Flight tests have been made to determine the longitudinal stability and control and stalling characteristics of a North American P-51H airplane. The results indicate that the airplane has satisfactory longitudinal stability in all the flight conditions tested at normal loadings up to 25,000 feet altitude. At Mach numbers above 0.7, the elevator push force required for longitudinal trim decreased somewhat because of compressibility effects. The elevator stick force per g in accelerated turns at the forward center-of-gravity position of 24 percent mean aerodynamic chord above 250 miles per hour was in excess of the required limits at both 5,000 and 25,000 feet altitude. The longitudinal-trim-force changes due to flaps and power were small, but the rudder-trim-force change with power change was high. The stalling characteristics in all the conditions tested were satisfactory...There was ample stall warning and recovery was always normal and prompt.*[10]

The Navy Grumman F6F-3 Hellcat

Navy Grumman F6F-3 Hellcat

NASA Langley Research Center via Larry Loftin

Jack also test flew another legendary WWII fighter in handling and performance studies, the Navy Grumman F6F-3 Hellcat. The Hellcat was rugged, provided more than adequate protection for the pilot, and had overwhelming firepower. The NACA flight studies helped the Navy to maximize the performance and handling characteristics of the airplane, which was ultimately responsible for more than half of all US Naval aerial victories scored in the Pacific. "Few changes were made in this outstanding aircraft in its operational lifetime, and by March 1945, the production rate reached 605 aircraft per month with an unbelievable unit price of $35,000. Certainly the Hellcat was one of the most successful fighters of the war, and one that required the least modification with service use of any such aircraft ever produced. The F6F-3 investigated by the NACA was the number 2 production aircraft. The only criticism of the F6F-3 was in relation to the lateral controls that were thought to be somewhat heavy. This was corrected in a modification which appeared on the F6F-5, an advanced version of the Hellcat."[11] Reeder's piloting skills were called upon for flight research studies of the longitudinal stability and control characteristics of the Hellcat. The NACA report to the Navy (co-authored by Reeder) summarized the findings:

> *At the request of the Bureau of Aeronautics, Navy Department, flight measurements were made of the handling qualities of an F6F-3 airplane. Thirty flights were made covering the period from February 1 to May 15, 1944.*[12]
>
> *In general, the pilots were favorably impressed with the longitudinal stability and control of the F6F-3 airplane. They considered it an easy airplane to fly. The control forces in abrupt and steady maneuvers were satisfactory. Also, the airplane was very easy to land. The results of the tests described herein showed the following details concerning the longitudinal stability and control of the F6F-3 airplane.*
>
> *The short-period longitudinal oscillations of the F6F-3 airplane were completely damped within one cycle.*
>
> *The neutral point (stick fixed) in the gliding condition varied from 36 percent mean aerodynamic chord at a lift coefficient of 0.2 to 39 percent mean aerodynamic chord at a lift coefficient of 1.0. Application of rated power (climbing condition) had a destabilizing effect above a lift coefficient of 0.4 that increased with increase in lift coefficient. In this condition the neutral point was located at 31.5 percent mean aerodynamic chord at a C_L of 1.0. At lift coefficients below 0.4, application of power appeared to have a*

> *small stabilizing effect.*
>
> *The use of flaps had a destabilizing effect. The stick-fixed neutral point in the landing condition varied from 35 percent mean aerodynamic chord at a C_L of 0.8 to 37 percent mean aerodynamic chord at a C_L of 1.4. The effects of power and flaps combined to make the wave-off the least stable condition tested.*
>
> *The stability with stick free was less than stick fixed. The difference between stick-free and stick-fixed stability increased with increase in lift coefficient.*
>
> *The stick force per g in maneuvers was satisfactory (3 to 8 pounds per g) at 3000 feet altitude for a center-of-gravity range between 29.9 and 33.2 percent mean aerodynamic chord. The desirable center-of-gravity range at 20,000 feet altitude lies between 26.6 and 30.5 percent mean aerodynamic chord.*
>
> *The elevator provided adequate control in takeoff at the most rearward center of gravity tested.*
>
> *The elevator power in landing was sufficient to effect three-point contact with the center of gravity aft of 21.5 percent mean aerodynamic chord.*
>
> *The longitudinal trim changes due to power and flaps were within the specified limits.*
>
> *The elevator trim tab was sufficiently powerful to trim the airplane as desired throughout the speed range in all flight conditions except below 120 miles per hour in the landing condition.[13]*

The Bureau of Aeronautics also asked the NACA to perform flight evaluations to determine the stalling characteristics of the Hellcat. Jack also performed these evaluations and his conclusions summarized in the NACA report:

> *1. Stall warnings existed in steady flight for the gliding, climbing, and landing conditions in the form of increased vibration, a duct howl in the power-off conditions, and gentle buffeting. The buffeting is not a reliable warning as it is obtained only if the stall approach is very slow. No stall warning existed for the approach or wave-off conditions.*
>
> *2. The initial roll-off was mild in most cases and could be checked by the use of ailerons and rudder. In cases where little or no control was used after the initial roll-off, mild rolling, and pitching oscillations set in and continued through the stall.*
>
> *3. In accelerated flight, stall warning was afforded by buffeting of the entire airplane. The resultant pitching and rolling oscillations, as well as the final roll-off, were mild and easily controllable.[14]*

During the latter stages of WWII, swept-wing technology became one of the breakthrough concepts for high-speed flight, and existing design guidelines had to be updated as new problems were encountered along with the benefits of swept wings. In particular, handling qualities and stall characteristics of swept-wing aircraft could be markedly different than the conventional unswept configurations—to the point of being unsatisfactory. Accordingly, the NACA, industry, and the military initiated programs to explore the advantages and problems of swept-wing aircraft.

The Bell L-39

Bell L-39 swept-wing research aircraft at the LMAL. Note the P-51D wing flow test aircraft at upper left.

NASA Langley Research Center

Jack Reeder participated in flight studies of the research airplane, which utilized the fuselage of the P-63 King cobra design and was the first American aircraft to incorporate the swept wing configuration conceived by NACA Langley (later NACA Ames) engineer Robert T. Jones. At Langley, Jack worked with engineers to correlate wind-tunnel data and projected flight characteristics of the L-39 with flight data. Results of these studies were summarized as follows:

> *Flight tests have been conducted to determine the lateral and directional stability and control characteristics of an airplane on which the wing panels are swept back 35°. For these tests, the wings were equipped with slots extending from 40 to 80 percent of the span of the sweptback wing panels measured from the inboard end. Wind-tunnel tests were made of a model of the airplane and wherever possible the flight and wind tunnel data have been compared.*
>
> *The directional stability was found to be positive with flaps up or down at all speeds tested. A large increase in dihedral effect with decrease in speed was noted, and the agreement between flight and wind tunnel measurements of dihedral effect was excellent except at high normal-force coefficients. Oscillations of the airplane and rudder resulting from abrupt deflection and release of the rudder were satisfactorily damped in all cases.*

Jack Reeder flight testing the Bell L-39 swept-wing research aircraft.
NASA Langley Research Center

The rolling motions involved in the oscillations were greater than normal, however, and the ailerons tended to float in phase with the sideslip angle. Flight and wind tunnel measurements of the aileron rolling effectiveness expressed by the rate of change of the rolling-moment coefficient with total aileron angle were in excellent agreement. The maximum values of the wing-tip helix angle reached in rudder fixed aileron rolls were low. At low speed the high dihedral effect caused a considerable reduction in the values that could be obtained."[15]

Navy Grumman XF8F-1

Towards the end of World War II, Jack evaluated the stability and control characteristics of the excellent Navy Grumman XF8F-1 Bearcat prototype piston-engine, high-performance, single-engine fighter as well as its production variants. One of his recommendations to Grumman was that the production aircraft be modified with a taller vertical tail.

NASA Langley Research Center via Larry Loftin)

Towards the end of the war, Jack evaluated the stability and control characteristics of the excellent Navy Grumman XF8F Bearcat prototype piston-engine, high-performance, single-engine fighter as well as its production variants. The aircraft, however, entered service too late to see any combat in World War II. It served with the Navy both at Naval Air Stations and aboard aircraft carriers until the early 1950s when it was replaced by the first generation of jet fighters. Reeder and project engineer H. L. Crane summarized Langley's involvement with the NACA Bearcat flight-test program as follows:

> *This paper presents the results of flight tests to determine the lateral and directional stability and control characteristics of the Grumman F8F-1 airplane with three vertical-tail configurations. The data presented herein have no bearing on the performance characteristics of the airplane, which were not measured but which were considered to be exceptionally good. The conclusions reached regarding the lateral and directional stability and control characteristics may be summarized as follows:*
>
> *It was found that the directional stability was poor with the production vertical tail. Addition of a 12-inch extension to the vertical fin and rudder produced a desirable improvement in directional stability and control characteristics. However, further enlargement of the vertical tail would be required to make the directional stability satisfactory in all respects.*
>
> *There was a tendency for the rudder control force to overbalance at large angles of right sideslip with the modified vertical tails. There was no such tendency with the production tail configuration that included a dorsal fin. It was concluded that the dorsal fin should have been retained on the modified vertical tails.*
>
> *The aileron control characteristics were better than those of many comparable airplanes that have been tested. However, the ailerons did not satisfy the Navy requirements for satisfactory flying qualities with regard to either control forces or rolling effectiveness.*
>
> *The power of the rudder trimming tab proved to be inadequate and the tab should be enlarged and/or be provided with an increased deflection range.*[16]

Based on these and other evaluation comments, the Bearcat was modified, including the introduction of a taller vertical tail.

In addition to assessing high-performance fighter aircraft during World War II, Reeder gained considerable experience performing research flights in late war Navy dive-bombers, including the Curtiss SB2C-1 Helldiver, which served as a replacement for the venerable Douglas SBD Dauntless during the latter years of the war in the Pacific. Specifically, he flew research missions in the SB2C-1 in 1944 to evaluate improvements in the aircraft's control system aimed at enhancing maneuverability. These included evaluations of modifications in the airplane's elevator system and the addition of wing-tip slots on the aircraft. Reeder and engineer Maurice D. White in an official NACA Memorandum Report later described the elevator system flight tests:

> *Three sets of elevators with various combinations of section contour, balancing tabs, bob weights, and control-system mechanical advantage were tested on an SB2C-1C airplane in an attempt to improve the elevator control-force characteristics in maneuvers. An arrangement was developed which with a 3-pound bob weight gave a variation of maneuvering stick forces of 6 to 18 pounds per g acceleration over the operating center-of-gravity range of 33.2 to 23.8 percent mean aerodynamic chord; this arrangement consisted of elevators having a nose contour less blunt than that of the production elevators, beveled trailing edges, a geared balancing tab with a linkage ratio of -0.33, and a control-system mechanical advantage that gave stick forces 22 percent less than that of the production arrangement for a given hinge moment. For the production elevators with the standard control system and a 5-pound bob weight the variation in maneuvering stick forces over the operating center-of-gravity range was 5 to 24 pounds per g. A set of elevators was tested that provided further reduction in the value of variation of elevator hinge-moment coefficient with elevator deflection, in an effort to obtain stick forces within the desired limits of 3 to 8 pounds per g over the operating center-of-gravity range. These elevators in conjunction with an 8-pound bob weight were found to provide a stick-force variation with center-of-gravity position in steady turns of about this magnitude, but the control was considered very objectionable by the pilot because it resulted in involuntary over control during takeoffs and rapid elevator movements. Because of this consideration no reduction in the variation of maneuvering forces with center-of-gravity position below that given by the improved arrangement mentioned previously was possible.[17]*

Reeder and engineer M. D. White in an official NACA Memorandum Report summarized the wing-tip slot flight evaluation tests as follows:

> *Flight tests have been conducted on an SB2C-1 airplane to determine the effects of the wing-tip slots on the flight characteristics of the airplane. The results indicate that in stalls in all flight conditions with the slots closed and covered with doped fabric and the wing leading edge smoothed, slightly higher values of the maximum normal-force coefficient were obtained than with the production arrangement where the slots were opened when the landing gear was extended. The production slot arrangement did reduce the*

maximum rolling velocities and accelerations experienced in the stall roll-off. The aileron control characteristics and the longitudinal stability of the airplane at low speeds were unaffected by the slot arrangement and it appears that, neglecting the effect of the difference in weight due to the slots, the takeoff performance will also be unaffected by the slot arrangement.[18]

British Supermarine Spitfire Mk. VII

British Supermarine Spitfire Mk. VII high-altitude fighter flight evaluated by Jack Reeder at Langley during World War II.

NASA Langley Research Center

While flight testing allied warplanes during World War II, Reeder also had the opportunity to evaluate two British warplanes pressed into service by the Royal Air Force: the Supermarine Spitfire Mark (Mk.) VII and DeHavilland F-8 Mosquito. The Spitfire Mk. VII design consisted of a basic Spitfire Mk. V fuselage, but had elongated wing tips for high altitude flying. The British had become weary of high flying German Junkers Ju-86 reconnaissance aircraft that began routine reconnaissance flights over the British Isles and to monitor British defenses on the island of Malta in the Mediterranean Sea. The Junkers Ju-86 was equipped with a pressurized cabin to enable its crews to comfortably operate the aircraft and complete their important mission at high altitudes. Once the RAF employed the Spitfire Mk. VII as a high-altitude interceptor, the Junkers Ju-86s were easily dispatched by the nimble spitfire, despite the lack of a pressurized cockpit for its pilot.

At Langley, Jack flew the Spitfire Mk. VII in studies to determine the aerodynamic effects of placing canvas coverings over the aircraft's outer wing gun ports, a common practice that the British exercised during the war with their Spitfires and Hawker Hurricane fighters to prevent dirt or mud from accumulating in the ports. When the guns were fired, the cannon shells or machine gun bullets simply fired through or pierced the canvas without interruption of their trajectory. Of course this practice contributed to aerodynamic drag on the design of the aircraft and according to W. Hewitt Phillips, one of NACA Langley's top aeronautical engineers at the time, "some of the Spitfires stalled in flight after firing their cannons/machine guns due to the rough protrusions left on the leading edge of the wings."[19] Knowledge gained from these studies helped the British to prevent this from happening throughout the last two years of the war in Europe. The remainder of the NACA flight studies of the Spitfire Mk. VII included handling and performance evaluations as well as pilot familiarization studies.

DeHavilland F-8 Mosquito

Jack also test flew the DeHavilland F-8 Mosquito, an all-wooden design, that was operated by the RAF as a bomber. The Mosquito, though an excellent bomber, had no defensive armament and its flight crews relied on its speed and agility when pursued by German fighters and night fighters. Jack flew the Mosquito in stability, control, and pilot familiarization studies.

British-built DeHavilland F-8 Mosquito twin engine bomber evaluated by Reeder in stability and control studies.

(NASA Langley Research Center)

Boeing Superfortress and the Consolidated Liberator

Boeing B-29 Superfortress used by NACA Langley for drop model testing.

NASA Langley Research Center

Consolidated B-24D Liberator used for model drop testing at NACA Langley during World War II. The large hangar building to the right was a balloon/dirigible hangar used by the Army Air Service following World War I to house balloons and dirigibles used to train Army air crews in operating Lighter-Than-Air (LTA) craft.

NASA Langley Research Center via Larry Loftin

Drop model mounted on underwing pylon beneath Boeing B-29 Superfortress at NACA Langley.

NASA Langley Research Center via Larry Loftin

Reeder also had the opportunity to test fly several American four-engine "heavy" bombers, including the Boeing B-17G Flying Fortress, Consolidated B-24D Liberator, and two different versions of the Superfortress (one used for studying basic handling and performance characteristics and the other used for special drop-model testing projects). The Flying Fortress, Liberator, and drop-model version of the Superfortress flown by Reeder at Langley performed numerous research flights in which "free-fall" drop models were dropped from either the bomb bays of the airplanes (B-17G and B-24D) or underwing pylons located near the fuselage of the aircraft (B-17G and B-29) at high altitudes for the study of aerodynamics in excess of Mach 1 (the speed of sound) through radar monitoring and telemetering. Most of these flights were performed over the Plum Tree Island bombing range near Langley. The information obtained from these flight studies proved to be critical because wind tunnels at the time did not have the capability to run at transonic or supersonic speeds.

Douglas A-26 Invader attack bomber

Douglas A-26 Invader flown by Jack Reeder in engine nacelle drag reduction studies at NACA Langley.

(NASA Langley Research Center)

Following the war, data from slotted-throat wind tunnels provided more accuracy and control of test conditions. Jack also flew important engine nacelle drag reduction flight studies in the twin-engine Douglas A-26B Invader attack bomber that also appeared in the European and Pacific skies during the latter stages of the war.

During his busy World War II flight research experiences, Reeder became better acquainted with his boss, Mel Gough, and Herbert (Herb) Hoover. Hoover became one of Jack's best friends. Their friendship, however, would later come to a tragic end as described later in this book. Hoover was raised in Knoxville, Tennessee. He was a Mechanical Engineering graduate from the University of Tennessee, class of 1934, and entered the Army Air Corps. He later flew for the Standard Oil Company in South America, transporting equipment, staff, and medical patients to and from various facilities and establishments. Hoover journeyed back to America in December 1940, and landed a position as a research pilot with the NACA at Langley. Among Herb's early accomplishments at Langley was his performance of precedent-setting flight research in severe thunderstorms in the first of the NACA's "storm chaser" aircraft, the Lockheed XC-35, which also happened to have a pressurized cabin for high-altitude flight. Other important contributions by Hoover included his flight research studies in the Army Bell P-39 Airacobra fighter and Navy Curtiss SB2C Helldiver dive bomber. Reeder also came to know test pilot William (Bill) Gray, Jr. well and developed a close friendship with him as well.

The Check-Out Process

Before test flying aircraft in the research environment at Langley, there was a particular mental routine that a pilot had to perform before commencing an evaluation flight. Reeder described this mindset or "check-out" process in detail:

> *Flying a large number of different types of aircraft and retaining currency in the various types requires that the research pilot be able to check himself out in an aircraft without dual instruction. Such a self check-out is an obvious necessity in the case of single seat*

fighters, but is highly desirable in other types as well. The process involves the following steps:

a) Thorough study of pilot's handbook with particular attention to aircraft systems, cockpit layout, pilot's notes, and performance characteristics.

b) Detailed discussions with other pilots who have flown the aircraft.

c) Cockpit familiarization that involves sitting in the cockpit, sometimes for several hours, memorizing the location and actuation procedures for the various system controls. Then, as now, there were no rigid standards governing cockpit design and layout. Thus, the cockpit layout of each aircraft type differed in some degree from that of all other types.

d) A brief flight test of the aircraft to determine the stall speed for various configurations such as flaps and landing-gear down and up, as well as power on and off. Other important speeds such as approach and climb speeds can usually be related to the stall speed by well-known approximate factors. Execution of several definitive maneuvers to provide useful information on the longitudinal and lateral-directional stability, control, and handling qualities of the aircraft. Thus, a short, well-planned flight test of perhaps an hour and a half duration, can provide the experienced research pilot with a clear picture of the basic flight characteristics of what had previously been a totally strange aircraft.

e) Maintenance of a notebook on each of the various types of aircraft flown. In addition to a summary of the results of the flight tests described above, detailed check lists for all phases of flight from pre-engine-start to engine shut-down following landing should be developed. The pilots reviewed these check lists before each flight. Although all pilots were urged to memorize and use these check lists, many situations were experienced in which time did not permit their detailed use. For example, traffic congestion in the landing pattern might severely restrict the pilot's available time; or in many cases, it was difficult to taxi to the end of the runway for takeoff and go through the check list in detail without over-heating the engine. Thus, use was frequently made of easily-remembered phonetic-type check lists to ensure proper setting of the various critical controls. One of the simplest of these phonetic check lists was 'GUMP' which translates as follows:

G—Gas, proper tank selection and use of boost pump.

U—Undercarriage, wheels down for landing.

M—Engine Mixture Setting.

P—*Propeller Pitch Setting.*

A somewhat more detailed phonetic check list that Reeder recalls using was: 'All Good Pilots Must Land Fine', which translates as follows:

A—*Correct Altimeter Setting.*

G—*Gas, proper tank selection, and use of boost pump.*

P—*Propeller Pitch Setting.*

M—*Engine Mixture Setting.*

L—*Landing Gear Position.*

F—*Wing and Cowl Flap Setting, and carburetor controls.*

Sometimes these phonetic checklists were printed on the instrument panel. Other check lists of this type were used but, the two cited above illustrate the technique...By following the steps outlined above, the intelligent, highly motivated, research pilot can maintain currency in a large number of different aircraft types.[20]

Transitioning from Piston-Engine Aircraft to the Jet Age

By the end of World War II, Jack had practically mastered the art of piloting and evaluating piston-engine high-performance military aircraft. However, the days of the piston-engine high-performance fighter were waning as military interests turned to jet-powered flight. Jack's finely honed engineering/piloting skills would be called upon again by the NACA in an effort to provide engineering design data for the complex phenomena associated with this new progressive form of flight, and to help the United States maintain a position of aeronautical supremacy over emerging threats to global peace and security.

During his World War II flight research experiences, Reeder became better acquainted with his boss, Mel Gough (left), and developed lasting friendships with several fellow test pilots at Langley. Jack's boss Herb Hoover (second from left) became one of Jack's best friends. The pilots were posing for a photo in front of an NACA Langley P-47D Thunderbolt. Reeder can be seen in the middle along with test pilots Stefan Cavallo and Bill Gray to the right of Reeder.

NASA Langley Research Center via Jack Reeder

Jack Reeder (third from left standing) and Boeing B-29 Superfortress flight test crew.

NASA Langley Research Center via Larry Loftin

Chapter Three Notes

1. Loftin, Laurence K., Jr. (Unpublished Manuscript, July 1986). A Research Pilot's World as Seen from the Cockpit of a NASA Engineer-Pilot, Chap. 1, pp. 1-2.2.

2. Ibid., Chap. 1, pp. 3-5.

3. Ibid., Chap. 3, pp. 12-13.

4. Ibid., Chap. 3, p. 14.

5. Ibid., Chap. 3, pp. 14-15.

6. Interview with Todd Hodges (June 16, 2006). Yorktown, Va.

7. Kraft, Christopher C. Jr., Goranson, Fabian R., and Reeder, John P. (February 1953). National Advisory Committee for Aeronautics (Technical Note 2899): Measurements of Flying Qualities of an F-47D-30 Airplane to Determine Longitudinal Stability and Control and Stalling Characteristics. Langley Aeronautical Laboratory, Langley Field, Va. NACA, Washington, p. 1.8.

8. "Jack Reeder Retires From NASA-Langley". *Virginia Aviation*, Oct.-Dec. 1980. Commonwealth of Virginia Department of Aviation, p. 1.

9. Ibid.

10. Kraft, Christopher C. Jr. and Reeder, J. P. (no publication date). National Advisory Committee for Aeronautics Research Memorandum for the Air Materiel Command, U.S. Air Force (NACA RM No. SL8B24): Measurements of the Longitudinal Stability and Control and Stalling Characteristics of a North American P-51H Airplane (AFF NO. 4-64164). National Advisory Committee for Aeronautics Langley Memorial Aeronautical Laboratory, Langley Field, Va., pp. 1 and 9.11.

11. Loftin, Laurence K., Jr. (Unpublished Manuscript, July 1986). A Research Pilot's World as Seen from the Cockpit of a NASA Engineer-Pilot, Chap. 5, p. 6.

12. Williams, Walter C. and Reeder, John P. (February 13, 1945). National Advisory Committee for Aeronautics Memorandum Report for the Bureau of Aeronautics, Navy Department: Flight Measurements of the Flying Qualities of an F6F-3 Airplane (BUAER NO. 04776) I – Longitudinal Stability and Control. National Advisory Committee for Aeronautics Langley Memorial Aeronautical Laboratory, Langley Field, Va., p. 1.

13. Ibid., pp. 13-15.

14. Williams, Walter C. and Reeder, John P. (February 13, 1945). National Advisory Committee for Aeronautics Memorandum Report for the Bureau of Aeronautics, Navy Department: Flight Measurements of the Flying Qualities of an F6F-3 Airplane (BUAER NO. 04776) III – Stalling Characteristics. National Advisory Committee for Aeronautics Langley Memorial Aeronautical Laboratory, Langley Field, Va., pp. 4-5.

15. Sjoberg, S. A. and Reeder, J. P. (January 1948). National Advisory Committee for Aeronautics Technical Note No. 1511: Flight Measurements of the Lateral and Directional Stability and Control Characteristics of an Airplane Having a 35° Sweptback Wing with 40-Percent-Span Slots and a Comparison with Wind-Tunnel Data. Langley Memorial Aeronautical Laboratory, Langley Field, Va. NACA, Washington, p. 1.

16. Crane, H. L. and Reeder, J. P. (no publication date). National Advisory Committee for Aeronautics Research Memorandum for the Bureau of Aeronautics, Navy Department: Flight Measurements of Lateral and Directional Stability and Control Characteristics of the Grumman F8F-1 Airplane (Ted No. NACA 2379). NACA RM No. L7L31. National Advisory Committee for Aeronautics Langley Memorial Aeronautical Laboratory, Langley Field, Va., p. 1.

17. White, Maurice D. and Reeder, John P. (no publication date). <u>National Advisory Committee for Aeronautics Memorandum Report for the Bureau of Aeronautics, Navy Department: Flight Investigation of Modifications to Improve the Elevator Control-Force Characteristics of the Curtiss SB2C-1C Airplane in Maneuvers (TED NO. NACA 2333)</u>. NACA MR No. L5D04a. National Advisory Committee for Aeronautics Langley Memorial Aeronautical Laboratory, Langley Field, Va., pp. 1-2.

18. White, M. D. and Reeder, J. P. (November 13, 1944). <u>National Advisory Committee for Aeronautics Memorandum Report for the Bureau of Aeronautics, Navy Department: Effect of Wing-Tip Slots on the Stalling and Aileron Control Characteristics of a Curtiss SB2C-1 Airplane (MR No. I4K13)</u>. National Advisory Committee for Aeronautics Langley Memorial Aeronautical Laboratory, Langley Field, Va., p. 1.

19. Interview with W. Hewitt Phillips (June 13, 2006). Hampton, Va.

20. Loftin, Laurence K., Jr. (Unpublished Manuscript, July 1986). <u>A Research Pilot's World as Seen from the Cockpit of a NASA Engineer-Pilot</u>, Chap. 3, pp. 15-18.

Chapter Four
The Jet Age

In 1946, Jack and fellow test pilot Bill Gray traveled to the Bell Aircraft facility in Buffalo, New York, to check out the XS-1 which was being readied for its first test flights.

Jack Reeder via Larry Loftin

One of the thirteen Bell YP-59A Airacomet jet fighter prototypes was tested for drag cleanup in the Full Scale Tunnel in 1943.

NASA Langley Research Center

During the final years of World War II, several of the combatant nations made tremendous strides in the development of turbojet powered aircraft, and in 1944 several jet combat aircraft became operational. In Europe, Germany deployed the Messerschmitt Me-262 Schwalbe (Swallow), as well as the Arado AR-234 Blitz. Although deployment strategies severely hindered the ultimate impact of these advanced weapons on the outcome of the war, the tremendous speed advantage they exhibited against Allied combat aircraft shook military leaders and precipitated an intense effort to develop similar capabilities. England also deployed the Gloucester Meteor in 1944, and although it did not see much combat duty over enemy territory, it was flown in an interceptor role to shoot down the dreaded V-1 buzz bombs that continually harassed residents of the British Isles during the closing months of the war. Inspired by the German success with the Me-262 design, Japan entered the jet race in 1945 with the development of the Nakajima Kikka, a jet fighter based on the Me-262 design. Two Kikka prototypes had made only two flights by the end of the war, and the aircraft never was put into production or operational service.

Bell YP 59-A

America entered the jet age with the development of the Bell P-59 Airacomet jet fighter. Shrouded under the utmost secrecy, the first P-59 made its initial flight at Muroc Dry Lake (now Edwards Air Force Base), California on October 1, 1942. One of the thirteen YP-59A prototypes underwent drag cleanup tests in the Full Scale Tunnel in 1943. Although the performance of the production P-59 was not spectacular (maximum speed of 413 mph at 30,000 feet), and it never got into combat, the airplane provided experience and training for personnel, and invaluable data for subsequent development of higher performance jet airplanes. The first operational U.S. jet fighter, the Lockheed P-80 Shooting Star, first flew in 1944 and production versions were deployed in 1945; however, the war ended before the P-80 could be used in combat.

XS-1-2 and its B-29 mothership on the ramp at Muroc, California. (NASA Dryden Flight Research Center)

NASA Langley Research Center

Clearly, the days of the piston-engine air superiority fighter were numbered, and NACA personnel and facilities had become deeply involved in ensuring that the performance and flying qualities of this new breed of jet aircraft would dominate the skies. In addition to participating in the development of specific aircraft at the request of the Army and Navy,

Langley planned and conducted fundamental studies of supersonic flight that provided the data and technical maturity to pursue major advances in speed and altitude. These contributions proved invaluable to the Nation's initiation of X-plane activities, regarded as a "golden age" of aeronautical innovation and accomplishments.

Langley test pilots Bob Champine (left) and Herb Hoover (right) pose beside the XS-1-2 aircraft at Muroc, California. (NASA Dryden Flight Research Center)

NASA Langley Research Center

The XS-1

By 1946, Jack Reeder had become a superb engineering test pilot with outstanding credentials, and he had gained the solid respect of high-ranking NACA officials within the agency. The prominence of Jack's professional capabilities was clearly defined when he was chosen by the NACA to serve as the first civilian test pilot to fly a new rocket-powered research aircraft that was being jointly developed by the Bell Aircraft Company, the U.S. Air Force, and NACA.[1] The airplane concept, designated the XS-

1, had been designed to penetrate and exceed the sound barrier. The XS-1 was being extensively tested in Langley's wind tunnels under the direction of Langley visionary John Stack, an engineer who would subsequently manage the NACA portion of the XS-1 test program.

Jack and fellow test pilot Bill Gray traveled to the Bell Aircraft facility in Buffalo, New York, in 1946 to check out the XS-1, which was being readied for its first test flights. Three XS-1 aircraft were built, and the Air Force and NACA agreed to split prime responsibilities and flight-test objectives between the first two airplanes. The first airplane, XS-1-1, would be flown by Bell and Air Force pilots, with a prime objective of achieving supersonic flight and breaking the sound barrier. The second ship, XS-1-2, would be flown mostly by Bell and NACA pilots to gather detailed engineering research data.

Unfortunately, the honor bestowed on Reeder by NACA with its selection for him to pilot XS-1-2 caused a serious personal dilemma for him. Jack and his wife, Frances, had talked to other prominent test pilots around the country who had already visited the primitive surroundings of the High Speed Test Flight Station at Muroc (which later became known as Edwards AFB). The Reeders, who were expecting the birth of their first child (daughter Shirley) at the time, did not like the prospects of living in the old Army barracks at Muroc used to house the flight-test personnel and their families at that time. Jack said "My wife and I didn't like the fact that so much sand would enter the houses through cracks under the doors and in the window emplacements. It would also get very hot and dry out there and I couldn't see raising my family out there in that kind of environment."[2] Consequently, after giving the opportunity much consideration, Jack turned down the offer to fly the XS-1 past the speed of sound, resulting in Herb Hoover becoming the second person—and the first civilian test pilot—to fly the "flying bullet" past the sound barrier.

The P-51H

Jack flew this P-51H (later redesignated F-51) at Langley in loads studies and evaluations of its reinforced fuselage and tail structures during the 1940s and early 1950s.

NASA Langley Research Center via Jack Reeder

Back at Langley, Jack and other NACA pilots were conducting some of the final flight tests of piston-engine holdovers from the war, while familiarizing themselves with the handling qualities of America's new jet aircraft, which were emerging in large numbers from the energized aircraft manufacturers for the Air Force and Navy. The last variants of famous World War II aircraft, such as the Navy F4U-5 Corsair and Air Force P-51D and P-51H Mustang, also made combat appearances in the Korean War. These aircraft were flown by Reeder to evaluate handling and performance characteristics.

North American F-82 Mustang Fighter

This North American F-82B Twin Mustang fighter loaded with a rocket model on its center underwing pylon and bomb-drop test models on its outer-wing pylons was test flown by Jack during the latter 1940s and early 1950s to evaluate the high-speed aerodynamic performance of rocket and bomb drop models.

NASA Langley Research Center via Larry Loftin

One of the more unique aircraft to be used in combat in the Korean War was the North American F-82 fighter. The prototype of the Twin Mustang series, the XF-82, arrived at Langley in 1948 for flight tests by Reeder to evaluate handling and performance characteristics, as well as an F-82B which was also test flown by Jack in rocket and bomb-drop tests to evaluate the high-speed aerodynamic performance of test models.

During those busy post-war years, Jack conducted extensive evaluations of high-priority prototype jet aircraft at the request of the services. Examples of the projects included the Air Force's P-80 Shooting Star (1948) and its later models, the F-80A and F-80B, which served in the Korean War. In 1949, Jack also evaluated the prototype of another Air Force straight-wing jet design that later saw duty in the Korean War, Republic YF-84A Thunderjet. The McDonnell F2H-1 Banshee was an early carrier-based Navy fighter design that was used for research studies over an 8-year period at Langley during the early 1950s. Reeder conducted flight tests of the F2H-1 at Langley aimed at improving the airplane's handling and stability characteristics. He also made familiarization flights in the Douglas F3D-2 Skyknight, a twin-engine two-seat night fighter and attack aircraft, used by the Navy and Marine Corps in Korea and Vietnam.

The North American B-45A Tornado

The North American B-45A Tornado (NACA-121) in which Jack completed 17 successful test flights. Tragically, Jack's fellow test pilot and best friend Herb Hoover was killed while flying this same airplane on August 14, 1952, when it came apart in mid-air.

NASA Langley Research Center

In 1948, Langley had received America's first jet-powered bomber, the B-45A Tornado, for flight testing from the North American Aircraft Company. German World War II jet bomber designs evaluated by the Allies after the war, such as the Arado 234 Blitz, as well as other German designs that were on the drawing boards but never made it into production heavily influenced the aircraft design. Reeder performed 17 very successful test flights involving transonic and maneuver load investigations in the B-45, which was designated NACA-121. Langley test pilots continued to perform research flights in the airplane until August 14, 1952, when Herbert Hoover was tragically killed when the aircraft came apart in mid-air.

Death of Herbert Hoover

Langley test pilot Herb Hoover boarding a North American F-51 Mustang fighter circa 1951. Hoover was Jack's boss and one of his best friends during and immediately after World War II.

NASA Langley Research Center via Larry Loftin

As described by Larry Loftin,

> "The accident involved an in-flight structural failure of the wings due to positive g-loads far in excess of the design value. John Harper was flying copilot with Hoover and was able to eject and land safely by parachute. Hoover also ejected but was apparently killed in the ejection process, possibly striking some part of the aircraft. Although the accident was meticulously investigated, the exact cause was never found. The longitudinal trim tab, however, was found to be 16 degrees out of position in the nose-up direction, as compared to the initial trim position for level flight, which suggests the possibility of some difficulty with the power-boosted control system. At that time, much was yet to be learned about the technology of powered controls. This type of control system has subsequently been widely and successfully used on many types of high-performance aircraft."[3]

Reeder had vivid recollections of the tragedy,

> "I was on vacation and received a phone call from Mel Gough, who said that Hoover had been killed in an accident. I flew out in a helicopter to view the wreckage that was strewn along the forest in an area north of the James River near Newport News. We later pieced together the wreckage in the flight hangar to try to determine the cause of the accident. It was a real blow to the flight research program at Langley and to NACA. I had lost one of my best friends."[4]

Following the accident, Jack was chosen to replace Hoover as Flight Operations Branch Head and test pilot James B. Whitten later took over Jack's old position as Section Head of the pilot's office. Reeder and Whitten, working in tandem, would go on to perform pioneering rotorcraft research during the same decade at Langley. As Head of Flight Operations and Chief Test Pilot at Langley, Jack's piloting activities had increased to demanding levels, and the managerial responsibilities of being responsible for flight operations posed additional challenges on a daily basis.

Grumman F9F2 Panther

Modified Grumman F9F-2 Panther flown by Jack in research studies to develop fly-by-wire concepts.

NASA Langley Research Center

Another Korean War jet fighter that served as a research workhorse at Langley was the Grumman F9F-2 Panther. Jack flew the modified F9F-2 in 1954 during a research project to develop fly-by-wire concepts. This unique test bed was the first jet aircraft in the world to incorporate an analog fly-by-wire control system, an early forerunner of today's advanced digital-fly-by-wire control systems used on high- performance military jet fighters and some commercial airliners. The pilot controlled the aircraft using a small side-stick controller located near the end of an arm rest at the side of the pilot, similar in layout to today's digital control systems. The side-stick controller was used in tandem with a rate-based automatic control system and irreversible electronic power control system. Decades later, this research came to maturity when NASA demonstrated a modern digital fly-by-wire system in flight tests of a specially designed Vought F-8C Crusader, known as the Digital Fly-By-Wire Testbed, at NASA Dryden Flight Research Center in Edwards, California. Such systems are now routinely used on such modern fighter aircraft as the Lockheed Martin F-16 Falcon, Boeing F/A-18 Hornet, and Lockheed Martin F-22A Raptor.

North American F-86 Sabre

NACA Langley's F-86A Sabre jet at Langley Field in 1953.
NASA Langley Research Center via Larry Loftin

In 1951, Langley initiated a decade of research on variants of the legendary Air Force F-86A Sabre jet. Jack performed handling and flight characteristics evaluations in the F-86A, which was highly instrumented and equipped with a special "wing shaker" device designed to provide data on flutter characteristics of swept-wing configurations at high speeds. As a result of the Langley flight research studies, the Sabre's maneuvering capability was dramatically enhanced. In the years to follow, Jack flew research studies on an advanced all-weather interceptor version of the F-86, the F-86D "Sabre Dog". The F-86D featured a deployable rocket-firing rack that dropped down under the fuselage for aerial combat. The aircraft was intended to intercept long-range Soviet bombers threatening the continental United States. The aircraft featured an advanced radar tracking system, which was evaluated by the NACA. The system was further modified and refined through flight instrumentation studies at Langley for improved target acquisition and tracking methods.

North American F-86D Sabre Dog flown by Jack in research studies. Note the "NASA" designation in the old NACA logo background on the tail. This unusual marking indicates that the aircraft was being test flown when NACA transitioned into NASA, most likely in October 1958.

NASA Langley Research Center

After the success of the X-1 program at Muroc in October 1947, American aircraft companies developed several other X aircraft, and flight testing of the X-series began to intensify at the renamed Muroc—Edwards Air Force Base. As flight testing activities grew at Edwards, Jack began to make frequent trips there to participate in flight tests with these advanced aircraft, and to visit with friends in the test pilot community.

One of Jack's best friends at Edwards was NACA/NASA standout test pilot Joseph A. Walker. Walker became a major figure of many of the early X-plane flight-test projects, and attained headline-grabbing attention from the American and international media in 1963 when he set an altitude record in the North American X-15 hypersonic research aircraft. Tragically, Walker later lost his life when flying chase in a NASA F-104N Starfighter that collided with one of the NASA/USAF North American XB-70 Valkyrie supersonic bomber/transport test aircraft in the skies over Edwards on June 8, 1966.

The Bell X-5 Variable Sweep Wing Research Aircraft

The Bell X-5 . (NASA Dryden Flight Research Center)

In the early 1950's, when the Bell X-5 variable-sweep research aircraft was being flight tested at Edwards, Joe Walker checked Reeder out in the aircraft and let him perform what became the shortest successful test flight ever flown in the aircraft. The X-5 was a design based on a German World War II jet aircraft, the Messerschmitt P.1101, developed by the Germans to explore the effect of wing sweep. The P.1101 was designed to permit manual variations of wing sweep between flights. In 1946, NACA Langley conducted extensive wind-tunnel studies of the X-5, which was being developed by the Bell Aircraft Company. Langley engineer C. J. Donlan recommended that a translating wing be incorporated in the design as a means of providing variable sweep in flight. The flight-test program officially commenced on June 20, 1951 when test pilot Jean Ziegler successfully performed the first test flight in the aircraft at Edwards.

During his flight in the X-5 at Edwards on July 16, 1952, Jack Reeder flew the X-5 to an altitude of 44,000 ft. and attained a speed of Mach 0.93, at 60° wing sweep. The flight lasted 1 hour and 8 minutes, and the speed achieved during the flight was remarkable given the fact that more powerful engines, originally intended for use on the airplane to provide it with supersonic capability, were never installed in the airplane.[5]

Boeing B-47A Stratojet

Boeing B-47A Stratojet taking off by means of a rocket assisted takeoff (RATO).

NASA Langley Research Center via Larry Loftin

In July 1952, Reeder had the privilege of flying a new swept-wing jet bomber that was slated for Air Force duty, the remarkable Boeing B-47A Stratojet. The airplane arrived at Langley from Boeing's aircraft plant in Wichita, Kansas, for evaluation flight tests that involved handling, control, and performance studies.

Vought F7U-1 Cutlass

Navy F7U-1 Cutlass at Langley for flight evaluations.
NASA Langley Research Center via Jack Reeder

During the early 1950s, researchers at Langley became interested in tailless airplane design concepts, and projects were initiated in the wind tunnels and flight to expand the knowledge and data base for such unique shapes. As part of this research undertaking, Reeder conducted flight evaluations of a new tailless, swept-wing jet fighter design that had entered service with the Navy, the Vought F7U-1 Cutlass. The Cutlass entered Navy service in May 1954 and was retired less than four years later.

Despite technical innovations such as the first naval aircraft to reach production that used afterburning engines, a pressurized cockpit and tricycle landing gear, the design had serious deficiencies. It was dramatically underpowered, had a faulty nose landing gear design that resulted in gear failures during carrier landings, exhibited gun-induced engine flameout tendencies, and poor stall/spin behavior at high speeds. By the end of its short operational career, the F7U had been responsible for the deaths of 4 test pilots and 21 naval aviators. In addition to wind-tunnel studies of the Cutlass design at Langley, a comprehensive flight research program was initiated. Extensive studies of F7U spin and spin recovery characteristics were conducted in the Langley Vertical Spin Tunnel. Jack Reeder's flight evaluations of the Cutlass to investigate the handling problems, together with wind-tunnel results and other studies led to later versions of the airplane with improved behavior.

During the 1950s, American civil and military aircraft leaders addressed the selection of advanced propulsion systems for high-speed aircraft. This focus centered on the relative advantages and disadvantages of turbojet engines or turboprop engines that used supersonic propeller concepts. A propeller designed for the supersonic range, coupled with a fuel-efficient turboprop engine, was viewed by many as a strong competitor to relatively fuel-hungry turbojet concepts. The Air Force and Navy committed to explore the potential of both systems. The military services, particularly the Air Force, sought an improvement in the speed and range of long-range interceptors and escort fighters for long-range strategic bombers. Research on supersonic propellers at Langley was led by John Stack, and included wind-tunnel, theoretical, and flight studies as discussed in the excellent historical review by John V. Becker.[6] The Langley flight research projects were led primarily by Tom Voglewede, Art Vogeley, and Jerry Hammack.

The Air Force's Wright Air Development Center (WADC) was conducting studies to develop feasible supersonic propellers with propeller manufacturers Hamilton-Standard and Curtiss-Wright. The performance capability of conventional propellers falls off rapidly at high speeds as the propeller tip speeds approach a Mach number of about 0.9 because of compressibility effects, severely limiting the maximum speed of the aircraft. Radically different propeller shapes are required to delay the performance loss and reduce loads on the propeller blades.

WADC engineers conceived a flight-test program to mature the supersonic propeller concept. The most powerful Allison turboprop engine at the time was chosen as a power plant, and a major modification to the Republic F-84F design was adopted for the research aircraft. The Navy also became interested in the concept and joined the program. In 1952, Republic was contracted for two prototypes that were designated XF-84H. An Allison XT40-A-1 turboprop engine that delivered 5,332 horsepower by means of a three-bladed prop mounted behind a huge spinner would power the aircraft. Initial flights of the XF-84H were conducted in 1955, exclusively at Edwards Air Force Base. The project was abandoned after the aircraft performance was found to be disappointing, never attaining supersonic flight. Moreover, pilots and ground crews did not anticipate the excruciating noise produced by the propeller. Personnel experienced severe headaches and nausea from the high noise levels encountered.

XF-88B Supersonic Propeller Testbed

McDonnell XF-88B landing with supersonic propeller feathered. NASA *Langley Research Center via Jack Reeder*

A second attempt to produce a supersonic propeller-driven fighter was again later explored by the Air Force when it convinced the McDonnell Aircraft Company to include an Allison XT-38 turboprop concept on one of its two new XF-88A fighter prototypes. The new airplane became know as the XF-88B, and it retained the two turbojets of the original design as well as the turboprop. Doubt voiced by critics still plagued hopes of producing an efficient, long-range supersonic aircraft. A joint program between the Air Force, Navy, and NACA was developed. The Air Force provided the XF-88B airplane and the test propellers and associated equipment, and the Navy provided the turbojets and the XT-38 turboprop engine, which was installed in the nose of the XF-88B to power the test propellers. The NACA originally intended to utilize either a B-45 or B-47 as flight research subjects.[7]

Jack Reeder preparing for a research flight at NACA Langley in the XF-88B in August 1956. The airplane is outfitted with a bulbous conical spinner and short bladed supersonic propeller. The flow survey rake mounted on the fuselage behind the propeller was used to measure propeller wake and thrust.

NASA Langley Research Center via Jack Reeder

Reeder was sent to pilot the XF-88B from the McDonnell aircraft manufacturing facility in St. Louis to Langley in May 1953 to commence a 5-year series of investigations to determine the practicality of the supersonic propeller. Various types of propeller blades were examined during the flight studies with two, three, and four blades evaluated at different stages.[8] In addition, various spinners were also test flown as part of the investigation. During the research flights, Jack would pilot the aircraft to an altitude of approximately 20,000 ft. using power from the turbojet engines. After reaching this altitude, he turned on the turboprop engine. The aircraft, according to Reeder, flew efficiently, reaching Mach 0.95 at approximately 30,000 ft.9 "The propellers were very thin at the tips, and gave efficiencies of about 83 percent, but were very noisy. Data were also obtained at low supersonic speeds with the airplane in dives," said Reeder.[10]

Jack Reeder (left) and Phil Houghton of the McDonnell Aircraft Company admiring the long supersonic propeller blades of the XF-88B.

NASA Langley Research Center via Jack Reeder

Art Vogeley, the project engineer for the XF-88B, later recalled on his experiences with the test program stating "The supersonic propeller was so noisy, that residents as far away as Richmond, Virginia, could tell when the thing was running."[11] He also spoke about how Reeder attempted to set a transcontinental speed record in the aircraft, flying from Edwards AFB to Langley, but was forced to land in St. Louis at the McDonnell plant due to technical problems. "We hoped we could set a world speed record with the airplane," said Vogeley.[12]

A total of 30 flights were made by Reeder in the XF-88B before the flight-test program was terminated. Unfortunately, interest in high-speed propellers had almost disappeared because of the advantages offered by high-performance and relatively maintenance free turbojet engines. However, design data derived from the Langley supersonic propeller research studies benefited the development of other advanced turboprop aircraft such as the civil Lockheed Electra and Navy Lockheed P-3 Orion, which is still in service today. Becker concludes "There was still hope that 500-600 mph transports might need transonic propellers, especially for long range, but with the advent of the Comet and the 707 this application also faded and the NACA high-speed propeller program ended with the transition to NASA."[13] A resurgence of interest in turboprops emerged in the 1980s, when world oil supply and cost issues served to force a re-examination by NASA and industry of more efficient power plants for transport aircraft.

Grumman F9F-7 Cougar

In 1954, a swept-wing version of the Grumman Panther, the F9F-6 Cougar, arrived at Langley from the Grumman aircraft plant in Bethpage, New York, for flight testing. Jack performed auto throttle evaluations in a later version of the aircraft, the F9F-7, as well as handling and performance tests. During the same year, Reeder made the trip west to Edwards AFB to participate in flight tests of the new delta-wing Air Force Convair YF-102 Delta Dagger, one of the first of the famous "Century" series of jet fighters developed during the 1950s and early 1960s. A later version of the Delta Dagger, designated the YF-102A, incorporated the area-rule concept conceived by Langley engineer Richard Whitcomb. Before incorporation of the area rule to the YF-102, pilots experienced difficulty traversing the sound barrier in the aircraft.

NACA Langley F9F-7 Cougar. Jack ferried the aircraft from the Grumman Bethpage plant in Long Island, New York, to Langley. The aircraft was used for carrier approach studies and pilot instrument needs, including tests of a new autothrottle system.

Langley Research Center via Jack Reeder

Vought F8U-1 Crusader

With the modification, the aircraft easily attained supersonic speeds. In 1956, Langley received a Vought F8U-1 Crusader for flight testing. The Crusader, a supersonic jet fighter that also incorporated the area rule, was developed for the Navy for use aboard aircraft carriers as an advanced fleet defender. The Crusader's wing incorporated a variable incidence feature that improved the landing approach visibility and takeoff qualities of the aircraft. However, the Crusader possessed severe mechanical and stability and control problems that jeopardized the progress of the developmental program. Setbacks included a series of crashes and delays in the flight-test program due to the inability of the wing to lock in the "down" position after takeoff. Control problems resulted in instability in high-speed maneuvers, which was the primary cause of a catastrophic in-flight disintegration of a production test aircraft in the skies above the Vought aircraft production facility in Dallas, Texas, in 1957.

Vought F8U-1 Crusader during flight tests at Langley.
Langley Research Center

To correct the airplane's unacceptable characteristics, Chance Vought, the Navy, and the NACA formed a working partnership. The NACA tasked Langley engineers William H. Phillips and Christopher C. Kraft, Jr. (Kraft later became Director of NASA's Manned Spacecraft Center) to assess the problems of the F8U and suggest potential solutions. An extensive research program was established at Langley to enhance the stability and control systems of the aircraft. This research program also involved wind-tunnel investigations to study lateral and directional stability at high angles of attack.

Reeder and fellow Langley test pilot Robert A. Champine flew research missions in the Crusader, including aerodynamic performance testing, formation flying, and target tracking studies. Reeder and Champine found the F8U-1 to be an "excellent" flying aircraft and correlation of flight and wind-tunnel data were good.[14] The pilots and researchers encountered the airplane wing "lock down" difficulty.[15] Flight tests also led to suggested modifications that corrected the "lock down" problem. Upon further analysis by researchers at Langley in combination with data generated from the Dallas incident, it was determined that serious problems still could be precipitated by the design of the aircraft's control system. The system was therefore modified to produce a direct link between the control stick and stabilizer deflection and was later incorporated in more advanced versions of the F-8 that remedied the instability problem in high-speed maneuvers.[17]

Grumman F11F-1 Tiger

Grumman F11F-1 undergoing tests at Langley
NASA Langley Research Center

In 1957, Langley received the first Navy jet fighter to use Whitcomb's area rule concept, the Grumman F-11F-1 Tiger. The F11F-1 arrived for testing at Langley from Grumman's Bethpage plant in Long Island, New York, in 1957. Reeder flew the airplane during studies aimed at correlating flight data with results from wind-tunnel studies of the area-rule principle.

The Voodoo and the Super Sabre

Jack Reeder landing the NACA F-101A Voodoo at Langley Field.
NASA Langley Research Center via Jack Reeder

During the late 1950s, Reeder test flew two other Air Force Century series jet fighters, the McDonnell F-101A Voodoo and North American F-100C Super Sabre. NACA and Air Force pilots found that the Voodoo performed well in the long-range interceptor/escort role. With a top speed of 980 mph at 36,000 ft., the NACA decided to use the Voodoo as a generator aircraft in sonic-boom studies at Langley.[18] The NACA F-101A flight research program provided valuable early data concerning the propagation and characteristics of sonic booms generated by military aircraft. The program also furnished the NACA with a database that would prove to be important for supersonic transport research. Jack and fellow Langley test pilot William L. "Bill" Alford flew similar sonic-boom flight research missions in an Air Force North American F-100C Super Sabre in 1957 at Langley.

North American F-100C Super Sabre used for sonic boom flights.
NASA Langley Research Center

During the flight program, Langley researchers also studied how the low-speed landing-approach flying qualities of swept-wing supersonic jet aircraft could be enhanced, and analyzed the Super Sabre's stability at high speeds. The Air Force, Langley, North American, and the NACA Ames Research Laboratory participated in a joint flight research program in which the Super Sabre's design was modified by incorporating a new, taller vertical tail and new wing sections.

The aircraft achieved flight speeds up to about Mach 1.39 in the flight tests, providing aircraft manufacturers with additional sonic-boom data that was useful for designers in the American supersonic transport program of the of the 1960s.

Bill Alford's Death

Bill Alford died in a tragic accident while conducting test flights of a pre-production model of the Royal Navy Blackburn NA.39 Buccaneer two-seat strike aircraft in England on October 12, 1959. The British had sought the advice of experienced NASA flight research pilots in evaluating the flying qualities of the Buccaneer, which had been designed using the area rule. Alford, who was piloting the airplane accompanied by a British flight-test engineer, was evaluating low-speed characteristics at low altitude (because of weather conditions) when the airplane departed controlled flight and crashed.[19] The two airmen were unable to eject from the aircraft because of the low altitude, and both perished in the crash. Jack Reeder recalled, "When John Stack, who managed flight research operations at Langley at the time, learned of the accident he broke down in tears."[20] Jack was subsequently sent by Langley as a replacement for Alford and he successfully completed the NASA portion of the Buccaneer flight-test program. The Buccaneer went on to serve successfully with both the Royal Navy and later the Royal Air Force.

Bill Alford's death had a profound effect not only on the NACA staff, but also on Jack's family. Being married to a test pilot was not easy for Frances Reeder by any stretch of the imagination. "There were moments when I was a little apprehensive. But actually, when Jack would leave to go to work every day, I did not ask him 'Are you going to fly today?' Sometimes he would know, or sometimes he would not know I guess. I really was not sure. A lot of days he did not fly. So I just did not ask. I just decided that was what he wanted to do and I would support him in the best way possible," said Mrs. Reeder.[21] Her unfettered support for Jack and his passion in life, being a test pilot, was clearly evident when Jack was offered the opportunity to fly the XS-1 at Muroc in 1946. Oldest daughter Shirley Reeder Randall said "When I grew older, I understood what it took to become a test pilot and I knew about the risks they took in doing their jobs. So I was also apprehensive sometimes about it. The worst time was when he was sent to England to take the place of Bill Alford who had been killed in the crash of the British Buccaneer aircraft. The whole family was fearful for my father and Mom became depressed during the flight testing of this airplane. When he left one morning to go over to England for the tests, I was certain that would be the last time I would see him alive."[22] However, Jack's superb engineering foresight and analytical skills came through once again, helping him to successfully complete the NASA portion of the Buccaneer flight tests and assuaging the family's deep apprehension concerning the flight-test program.

Over the years, the Reeder family developed a close association with the "family" of American test pilots and their respective families. "It was particularly hard when over the years, we saw our friends die. People like Herb Hoover, Bill Alford, and Joe Walker. That was particularly tough and hard to get over. These were people that we knew well. They had children and we went to picnics together, attended other family get-togethers, and basically grew up together. It was just an indication of how dangerous being a test pilot really was. I did not like my father being a test pilot at all because I had seen my friends' fathers die in accidents," said Shirley Randall.[23] Most of the Langley test pilots and many of the notable Langley engineers settled in the neighborhoods of Newport News close to the Hilton Village area and when news of such tragedies struck it deeply affected these communities as well. However, the one thing that separated Jack from many of the other test pilots was that he was "very safety conscious about everything," said Mrs. Reeder.[24]

Nevertheless, there were numerous memorable happy times spent together by these families and their test pilot fathers or husbands. The Reeders often had NASA Dryden test pilot Joe Walker as a guest to spend time with the family. He first started making visits to see the Reeders at their home in Hampton and later spent hours entertaining them by playing his steel guitar. "He was very good at it and a jolly fellow. We would see him whenever we would visit our best man, Maury White, in California also. It was a tremendous loss when he was killed in his flight accident," said Mrs. Reeder.[25]

Neil Armstrong

(From left to right) Carol Reeder, Apollo astronaut in training Neil Armstrong, Frances Reeder, and Shirley Reeder during a visit by Armstrong to the Reeders' home in Newport News, Virginia during the late 1960s.

NASA Langley Research Center via Jack Reeder

Mrs. Reeder also met all of the original seven Mercury astronauts through her husband's association with them and had the opportunity to socialize with Neil Armstrong, when he visited the Reeder family at their home in Newport News. Armstrong was taking part in rendezvous/docking, lunar excursion, and lunar lander training at NASA Langley at the time, prior to taking his historic first steps on the lunar surface in July 1969.

During the early 1960s, Jack made the track once again to Edwards to test fly one of the last Century series jet fighters, the sleek Lockheed TF-104G Starfighter, in standard handling and performance tests. The Starfighter, designed as a high-speed interceptor, would go on to set both altitude and speed records while in service with the Air Force.

In summary, Jack Reeder's environment at Langley in the early jet age was crammed with flight research projects of national importance. Personal opportunities for professional growth had been faced, and Jack had made critical decisions with his priorities always in the right order. With international recognition coming his way, his flight research contributions and managerial capabilities formed the basis for the next focus of his career. In 1960, NASA Headquarters decreed that undue duplication of flight research effort was occurring between Langley and the NASA Dryden Flight Research Center. In response, Headquarters transferred responsibility for all high-performance aircraft flight work to Dryden and directed Langley to lead V/STOL and rotorcraft flight studies.

Crowded flight research subjects in the NACA Langley West Area Hangar due to Hurricane Hazel in 1954. The number of flight research assets illustrates the amount of work the NACA had for its pilots at the time. Unfortunately, the number of flight research aircraft at Langley would rapidly dwindle over the nextseveral decades as a result of NASA's changing priorities.

NASA Langley Research Center

This decision had a tremendous negative impact on morale among Langley researchers, pilots, and flight operation staff that would be duplicated in the 1970s by another unpopular Headquarters decision to move rotorcraft flight work to the Ames Research Center.[26] As a result of the 1960 decision, Jack launched himself into his ongoing rotorcraft and V/STOL activities with even more energy.

Chapter 4 Notes

1. Interview with John P. "Jack" Reeder (March 21, 1994). Newport News, Va.
2. Ibid.
3. Loftin, Laurence K., Jr. (Unpublished Manuscript, July 1986). <u>A Research Pilot's World as Seen from the Cockpit of a NASA Engineer-Pilot</u>, Chap. 4, p. 10.
4. Interview with John P. "Jack" Reeder (March 21, 1994). Newport News, Va.
5. Ibid.
6. Becker, John V. (1980). <u>The High Speed Frontier: Case Histories of Four NACA Programs, 1920-1950</u>, NASA SP-445. National Aeronautics and Space Administration, Washington, DC.
7. Letter from Jack Reeder to Richard C. Koehnen, January 6, 1981, p. 1.
8. McDonnell Aircraft Corporation Release, "The XF-88B High Speed Propeller Research Airplane," April 29, 1953, Records of the National Aeronautics and Space Administration RG 255-RA-A7-4bl, National Archives Still Pictures Branch, College Park, Md.
9. Letter from Jack Reeder to Richard C. Koehnen, November 17, 1980, p. 2.
10. Ibid., p. 3.
11. Interview with Art Vogeley, "Flight Research at NACA/NASA Langley," March 24, 1994.
12. Ibid.
13. Becker, John V. (1980). The High Speed Frontier: Case Histories of Four NACA Programs, 1920-1950, NASA

SP-445. National Aeronautics and Space Administration, Washington, DC, p. 138.

14. Memorandum from Christopher C. Kraft, Jr., to NACA Langley Associate Director, "Pilot opinion of the overall flying qualities of the F8U-1 airplane," June 26, 1957, <u>NACA Flight Research on Vought F8U-1 Airplane</u> (unpublished document compiled by William H. Phillips), NASA Langley Research Center.
15. Ibid.
16. "Improvements in F8U Stability and Control and Operational Safety as a Result of NACA Research," <u>NACA Flight Research on Vought F8U-1 Airplane</u> (unpublished document compiled by William H. Phillips), NASA Langley Research Center.
17. Ibid.
18. William Green and Roy Cross, <u>The Jet Aircraft of the World</u>. Garden City, New York: Hanover House, 1955, p. 172.
19. Interview with John P. "Jack" Reeder (March 21, 1994). Newport News, Va.
20. Ibid.
21. Interview with Mrs. Frances Winder Reeder and Shirley Reeder Randall (March 20, 2006). Newport News, Va.
22. Ibid.
23. Ibid.
24. Ibid.
25. Ibid.
26. Mallick, Donald L. and Merlin, Peter W. (2003). <u>The Smell of Kerosene: A Test Pilot's Odyssey</u>, NASA SP4108. NASA History Office, Washington, D.C., p. 92.

Chapter Five
Whirly Birds

Cierva C-8 autogiro modified by rotorcraft pioneer Harold Pitcairn. This early rotorcraft, shown at Langley in this photo, served as an example of technology transfer from Europe (Spain) to the United States and made an appearance at the NACA's 1929 Engineering Research Conference held at Langley.

NASA Langley Research Center via Frederick Gustafson

NACA Langley engineer John B. Wheatley and the amazing American-built Kellett YG-1 autogiro.

NASA Langley Research Center

Army YR-4B undergoing tests in the NACA Langley Full-Scale Tunnel in October 1944.

NASA Langley Research Center

Although Jack Reeder accumulated extensive flight time and experience in conventional fixed-wing aircraft during his flying career, he became an international legend for his unparalleled expertise in rotorcraft and V/STOL aircraft. His contributions were among the earliest and most important for the rotorcraft community, especially in the field of handling qualities.

The path to practical rotorcraft flight had begun with the development of the autogiro. An autogiro is a rotary-wing aircraft that uses a propeller for forward motion and a freely rotating, unmotorized rotor for lift. The Spanish aeronautical engineer Juan de la Cierva invented the concept in the early 1920s. The autogiro differs from the helicopter in that the engine does not continuously move the rotor, as the engine on a helicopter does. The engine is connected to the prerotator and is engaged only before takeoff. The small tractor propeller at the front of the vehicle pulls the autogiro forward in flight. The forward motion causes the rotor to turn automatically. Like an airplane, the autogiro must have a takeoff run before lifting off. The engine drives the rotor blades at a high rate of speed before the machine can leave the ground. Once in the air, the rotors are disconnected from the engine, and the blades continue to revolve because of the air pressure against the bottom of the blades. The lift provided by the rotor, called autorotation, provides flight. The autogiro can climb or descend very steeply and descend vertically, but, it cannot climb vertically or hover over one spot like a helicopter.

Kellett YG-1 autogiro

Researchers and pilots at Langley had gained extensive experience with American autogiros built by the Kellet and Pitcairn companies during the 1930s. These designs were tested in Langley's wind tunnels and in flight.[1,2] When concepts for the first practical helicopters emerged, and the utility and potential applications of the helicopter became obvious, the NACA quickly moved to assess the technology, identify problems, and provide solutions.

Reeder's experience flying helicopters or "whirly birds", as they came to be known, began in 1944 when he was detailed by the NACA to the Coast Guard Station at Floyd Bennett airport in Brooklyn, New York for special training to perform test flights in the world's first practical helicopter, the Sikorsky YR-4B (Army designation) or HNS-1 (Navy designation). Aviation pioneer Igor Sikorsky designed the YR-4B/HNS-1 "Hoverfly". Sikorsky had become known throughout the world for his famous flying boats produced throughout the 1930s and had experimented with helicopter designs in his native Russia. After emigrating to the U.S., he formed his own company and proceeded to develop the first single-rotor helicopter, the layout of which became a world standard.

Army YR-4B and Navy HNS-1

Jack flight testing the Navy HNS-1 in March 1945. Note the cross.
NASA Langley Research Center

With his training and experience, Jack became the first NACA test pilot to attain full qualification to fly rotorcraft. His initial rotorcraft flight project at Langley involved flight testing the Navy HNS-1 in March 1945. The Army version (YR-4B) had already been tested in the Langley Full-Scale Tunnel in October 1944 to establish aerodynamic behavior and rotor characteristics, so some engineering knowledge of the aerodynamic characteristics of the helicopter was known.[3] Reeder worked with engineer Frederic B. Gustafson on the flight-test project. Gustafson had become the rotorcraft engineering "guru" at Langley, and became a legend within the rotorcraft community.

Army YR-4B undergoing tests in the NACA Langley Full-Scale Tunnel in October 1944.

NASA Langley Research Center

Working together, Reeder and Gustafson explored all aspects of the helicopter as a flying machine, quickly becoming two of the most experienced rotorcraft experts in the world. They jointly described the problems associated with the flying qualities of helicopters in a report published by the NACA in 1954:

> It has been suggested in the past that flying a helicopter is a new and difficult art. In its present stage of development the helicopter is different and more difficult to fly than most airplanes. The difficulty seems to arise from three sources: the helicopter has one additional control (collective pitch) to be operated; the power controls (collective pitch and throttle) must be used almost continuously in conjunction with flight controls during operations near the ground, chiefly because of the rapid variation of power required with airspeed in the speed range normally used in these operations; and, the helicopter has undesirable stability characteristics in forward flight which would not be acceptable in an airplane. Hovering flight also introduces a new and unique problem which is, however, somewhat analogous to formation flying with airplanes.
>
> The NACA has long been vitally interested in stability and control problems and in setting up requirements for the satisfactory stability and control characteristics for airplanes. We are now in the process of extending this work to cover the case of the helicopter. It is recognized that airplane requirements may not be applicable to helicopters in a specific manner but, nevertheless, the underlying reason for setting up the requirements applies to both airplane and helicopter. We feel that sooner or later the helicopter is going to have to meet requirements parallel to those for the airplane in order to reach its potential capabilities.[4]

In the flight tests, Reeder flew the HNS-1 in tests to investigate the rotor performance, and several different rotor blades were test flown to determine the most efficient designs and configurations. The stability and control characteristics of the rotorcraft were also evaluated. Jack's usual in-depth analysis and evaluation comments were evident in the official NACA flight-test notes:

> During the course of the performance tests, considerable flying was done at relatively high speeds, approaching the limits imposed by blade stalling. It was found quite difficult to hold steady conditions because of a strong tendency of the machine to diverge in pitch, creating the impression of balancing on a ball. This characteristic seemed far more pronounced with some of the rotors tested than with others, but was always troublesome. Upward pitching was most troublesome as it frequently precipitated or intensified stalling, which added to the difficulties because it increased the tendency to pitch up and was accompanied by rather violent periodic stick forces and vibration. The forward displacement of the control from trim necessary to check some of these pitching motions suggested that a short delay in applying corrective control would allow a maneuver severe enough that control would be lost. Although there seemed ample control to stop downward pitching, an uncomfortable amount of forward control was again required

in order to check the subsequent upward pitching. These characteristics suggested a pronounced type of instability.

The tendency to depart from the trim speed and the necessity of applying appreciable control deflection against a pitching maneuver involving acceleration, initiated either by control or by external disturbances, is apparent throughout the speed range normally used in forward flight. It becomes much less pronounced, however, at the lower speeds.

Shortly after the embryo pilot experiences forward flight, he is impressed with the necessity for having to constantly fly the helicopter. At first thought the reasons for this situation are not clear. It is common knowledge that a flapping rotor tilts to the rear if speed is increased, thus tending to cause the machine to return to the original speed. Wind-tunnel tests of the YR-4B fuselage have shown it to be unstable, but this instability is evidently outweighed by the rotor stability just discussed, in as much as measurements of stick position have shown that the stick does move forward to trim at increasing steady speeds. Furthermore, observation and measurements have indicated that the static stick-force gradient with respect to speed is small, but has been either unstable, neutral, or stable, depending upon the pitching moments of the particular blades and upon the bungee configuration, without greatly altering the pilot's overall impression of instability. The source of the difficulty, therefore, cannot be either stick-fixed or stick-free instability with speed.

The somewhat obvious conclusion is that the pilot's impressions are a result of the helicopter's instability with angle of attack. There are at least two logical sources for its instability with angle of attack. The first results from the flapping of the rotor. If the helicopter rotor is subjected to an angle-of-attack change in forward flight, then for constant rpm the advancing blades are subjected to a greater upward accelerating force than the retreating blades because the product of angle-of-attack change and velocity squared is greater on the advancing side. The resulting flapping motion will then tilt the disk in the direction of the initial change, which results in an unstable moment. This effect is a function of the tip-speed ratio and becomes more pronounced at higher speeds. The second source is the unstable fuselage.

It may be well to point out here that airplanes can and do exhibit instability with angle of attack at times, but this condition is recognized as unsatisfactory and is generally prevented by keeping the center of gravity sufficiently well forward."[5]

In regard to the helicopter's hovering characteristics, Reeder had the following thoughts: *"Hovering, of course, precedes and follows all forward flight and is the outstanding reason for the existence of helicopter types. We feel, however, that at present the problems associated with hovering in this particular type are more indefinite than in forward flight, that they tend to disappear with a little flight practice, and that they don't affect its general utility to the extent that limitations on night and instrument flying do.⁶*

Modifications and refinements were made to the helicopter's design as a result of the Langley wind-tunnel and flight research programs, and the YR-4B went on to perform admirably in the Search and Rescue (SAR) role, rescuing numerous downed allied airmen, with the Army in the Pacific Theater during the last year of World War II. Typical of the fundamental value of NACA evaluations, Reeder's flight experiences and data obtained while flying the HNS-1 were directly incorporated into the military specifications for flying qualities of helicopters.

Bendix Model K "Whirlaway"

Jack performing a demonstration flight in the Bendix Model K "Whirlaway" co-axial helicopter at Langley on January 6, 1948.

NASA Langley Research Center via Jack Reeder

Jack's special insights in flying helicopters yielded great benefits for the NACA and the rotorcraft industry in the years to come. Following his initial HNS-1 experiences, he had the opportunity to fly and evaluate truly unique rotorcraft designs such as the tiny Bendix Model K "Whirlaway" co-axial helicopter and the Teicher "Hummingbird" in 1947. Bendix Helicopters, formed by Vincent Bendix of washing-machine fame, produced the Bendix machine. The Model K had made its first flight in June 1945, with a rotor diameter of 25ft and a length of only 12.5ft. The configuration included two stacked co-axial rotors over a small, pod like nacelle with tricycle gear. In December 1947, the Whirlaway was acquired by Langley for flight demonstrations for NACA and Army officials, and Jack was asked to perform a demonstration flight in the rotorcraft on the morning of January 6, 1948. Jack had the following comments on the performance of this light rotorcraft design:

> *The machine was noticeably unstable directionally while hovering in a variable 10 mph wind. I flew the machine forward then, at speeds not exceeding 30 mph, and in the existing gusty wind the machine was objectionably unstable directionally. An uncomfortable amount of control seemed to be necessary to keep it headed in the right direction. Longitudinally, the machine also had instability similar to that of more familiar types, but seemed to present more of a problem, presumably because of reduced size and inertia. The machine was relatively free of vibration except during transition from forward flight and/or descent to hovering where all machines pick up a vertical vibration of short duration. The stick had no noticeable vibration nor was there any feed-back of forces into the stick during maneuvers. Feel was provided by centering bungees. The directional control, despite noticeably high friction on the ground, provided a well-graduated and positive control that was not difficult to use. The collective pitch control and throttle were easy and natural in operation.*[7]

Bell 47 Helicopter

At about the same time, Sikorsky produced another helicopter for the Navy, the HOS-1 or R-6 "Hoverfly II", and Jack performed a series of NACA evaluation tests on the rotorcraft. At that time, Bell also produced a new helicopter known as the Bell 47. In 1946, the Bell 47 became the first helicopter to be approved for civilian use, and it would go on to become a legend in the Korean War with the United States Army MASH (Mobile Army Surgical Hospital) units, transporting wounded soldiers from combat zones. The helicopter also became the first rotorcraft to successfully transmit signals for television broadcasts. Langley acquired a Bell 47 for flight tests and Reeder performed extensive handling and stability tests with the rotorcraft.

Bell 47 Helicopter flown by Reeder for flying quality studies.
NASA Langley Research Center via Frederic Gustafson

By the outbreak of the Korean War in 1950, helicopters were in widespread use by the military services. The application of rotorcraft in combat situations on a large scale began to revolutionize warfare and provided military commanders with great logistical flexibility. At the same time, NACA Langley's flight research pilots and engineers worked to improve and enhance emerging designs as well as provide data for designers of future rotorcraft.

During the emergence of rotorcraft testing at Langley during the 1950s, Jack worked closely with another test pilot at Langley, James B. Whitten. Whitten had become head of the pilots' section and had family ties to Langley Field's historic past. Whitten acquired his knowledge of flight from his father, an Army Air Corps pilot who flew at Langley Field during World War I. When World War II started, Whitten entered flight training with the U.S. Army Air Force, successfully completing his training and becoming a Training Command Instructor. He earned a degree in engineering from the Georgia Institute of Technology following the war and landed a job with the NACA at Langley in June 1947 as a research pilot. He productively served as a research pilot and teamed with Jack on many studies until his eyesight deteriorated and he was removed from flying status.

In 1950, Reeder and Whitten conducted flight research studies to determine the effects of changing the levels of damping in pitch and roll on the flight characteristics of a single-rotor, two-blade, two-seat rotorcraft known as the Army Bell H-13B. "In these tests the damping of the helicopter in pitch and roll was varied by means of a rate-sensitive automatic-control device from the amount present in the helicopter with the device inoperative to nearly three times that amount. Longitudinal stability and control characteristics that were unsatisfactory with the device inoperative were improved by increasing the damping of the helicopter and were judged as satisfactory when the device approximately doubled the damping. The tests tended to confirm the proposed requirements of NACA TN 1983 that, for satisfactory stability, the curve for normal acceleration in a pull-and-hold maneuver should become concave downward within 2 seconds of the start of the maneuver. The largest amount of damping tested resulted in correspondingly reduced rates of roll. Although noticeably low, these rates, however, seemed adequate to the pilots for normal flying."[8]

Navy Sikorsky HO3S-1

In 1951, Reeder and Whitten participated in pioneering rotorcraft flight research efforts when they performed several "blind flying" experiments in a Navy Sikorsky HO3S-1 helicopter that had been acquired from Naval Air Station Patuxent River, Maryland. During the flight tests, Whitten sat in the back seat and drew a curtain around him that eliminated visual cues outside the enclosure. Whitten flew the helicopter by reading the

Jack Reeder and James Whitten (hidden behind shower curtain) performing blind flying experiments in the NACA HO3S-1 helicopter.

NASA Langley Research Center via Frederic Gustafson

NACA Langley test pilots James Whitten and Jack Reeder confer with each other after test flying the Piasecki HRP-1 tandem rotor helicopter.

NASA Langley Research Center

instruments as Reeder, seated in the front seat, served as the spotter. The successful completion of the tests verified the feasibility of operating an advanced rotorcraft by instruments alone (something needed desperately for night operations). The helicopter made use of a Sperry guidance navigation system.

Piasecki HRP-1 "Flying Banana"

In that same year, Reeder and Whitten teamed again in unprecedented rotorcraft flight research when they tested and evaluated the world's first practical tandem rotor helicopter, the Piasecki HRP-1, which also became known as the "Flying Banana" by its Navy and Marine Corps crews. Handling and stability characteristics of the unique design were the primary interests during the tests.

In 1954, Reeder summarized the important flight research findings of the NACA at Langley from its rotorcraft program in his "Notes on Helicopter Flight Research" published by the NACA: "One of the more interesting phases of the performance tests concerned the limits imposed by blade stalling. Rotor blade stalling is encountered at the higher forward speeds of the helicopter because the retreating blades, encountering lower relative air velocities as forward speed increases, must have their angles of attack increased to progressively higher angles in order to carry their share of the lift. Thus, the angles of attack of the retreating sections approach and exceed that for the stall. The stall occurs first at the tip for powered flight and normal blade twist. Note that stalling could be expected to begin on the retreating side near the tip whereas the advancing side is well below the stall. As is well known, blade stalling effects have been and are now limiting the high speed of helicopters, both from the performance and controllability standpoints."[9]

Reeder also elaborated on the importance of the NACA's instrument flying research performed in rotorcraft assigned to Langley.

The need for good handling qualities is more important for instrument flying than for contact flying, since instrument flight is inherently more difficult. Since the helicopter's utility lies in its low-speed capabilities, it is logical that eventually it must be operable in instrument flight at very low speed. Accordingly, a program of instrument flying was undertaken to explore the problems throughout the speed range…The immediate impressions derived from the instrument flying were that excessive concentration and effort were required. It was soon apparent that a great amount of attention was being paid to control of heading. Furthermore, heading control became increasingly difficult as speed was reduced. A major reason for this difficulty is the fact that the rate of turn for a given bank angle goes up as speed is reduced and becomes quite high at the lower speeds for a helicopter. Inadvertent deviations in bank result in relatively large heading changes during the period the pilot is scanning the instrument panel, particularly when other corrections to flight attitude have to be made. Even at the higher cruising speeds of 65 to 70 knots, the errors in heading tend to be noticeably larger than for an airplane during instrument approaches. Thus, one reason is apparent why excessive concentration and rapid instrument scanning are required…We had not expected from visual flight experience that control of heading would demand so much of the pilot's attention. Our blind-flying experience has found it to be a major problem. Constant correction of heading is aggravating, tiring, and time consuming. It is logically concluded that the pilot's job would be much simpler if essential heading and longitudinal information could be combined into one instrument. A new instrument panel was laid out to include a commercial instrument, the Sperry Zero Reader, which does this by means of a cross-pointer instrument. In this instrument, a heading-error signal and bank-angle signal are normally combined in the indications of a vertical needle so that centering the needle by means of the lateral control causes the aircraft to turn to and maintain any selected heading if the helicopter has a sufficient degree of static directional stability. The horizontal needle of the normal instrument indicates longitudinal attitude or a combination of attitude and altitude if desired. It should be made clear at this time that this instrument does not in any way replace the normal flight instruments, for it does not indicate what the aircraft is doing, only how to do it. The subject instrument reduces the scanning and mental effort required in making a heading correction. Our flight results, when using a somewhat modified instrument to meet the needs of the helicopter, immediately showed a great reduction in effort required and a marked improvement in accuracy of heading control at low speed. Typical errors of perhaps 30 degrees during a particular maneuver at low speed were cut down to a few degrees when using the Sperry Zero Reader."[10]

Reeder also drew the following conclusions on flying single rotor and tandem rotor helicopters:

> *The research described has provided some basic knowledge with which to continue and expand various fields of research. Our present plans call for continuing the handling qualities studies with the single rotor and, more particularly, with the tandem rotor types. Also, our instrument flying program will continue, primarily with emphasis on the very low speed range. In addition, we hope to expand our instrument-flying efforts to include other helicopter configurations.*
>
> *The helicopter loads program also will continue with a study of landing loads for single-rotor and tandem types. The Visual Guidance Heading (VGH) program has been expanded in an effort to correlate blade-bending-moment levels with specific flight conditions and air turbulence. Vibration, a field in itself, is also under study in an active flight project.*
>
> *In conclusion, I might say that it is believed there has been very extensive progress in rotary-wing research in the past several years. Although our efforts are spread fairly thin, we hope to take an active part in future progress.*[11]

Reeder also flew several other unique helicopter designs throughout the latter 1940s and 1950s including the Kaman K-190 twin rotor and Kaman K-225 helicopter that was used to perform aerial spraying of farm fields; the Sikorsky S-52 (HO5S) Navy helicopter, which was the first helicopter produced in the United States to make use of metal rotor blades; and the Piasecki HUP-1 tandem rotor helicopter that saw service with the Navy.

Hiller Hornet

Jack's rotorcraft experiences were further expanded by an advanced design of the Hiller Corporation. Hiller produced two helicopters that utilized ram jets on the tips of the rotor blades for extra lifting efficiency, the Hornet (HOE) and YH-32. Reeder conducted evaluations of both designs, and the YH-32 was test flown at Langley during 1956–58. While these helicopters effectively demonstrated the lifting ability of ram jet-tipped rotor blades, their other performance characteristics proved to be inadequate, and excessive noise problems produced by the ram jets plagued the progress of the rotorcraft development programs.

Jack Reeder test flying the Hiller Hornet (HOE).

Hiller Corporation via NASA Langley Research Center via Jack Reeder

Jack also maintained an awareness of helicopter developments in other countries, and quickly accepted invitations to fly the machines. The French company Sud Aviation had developed the Sud-Ouest SO-1221 Djinn helicopter in the 1950s, powered by cold-jet compressed air ducted through the rotor blades and then expelled as compressed air through nozzles at the rotor tips. Jack traveled to France to conduct a familiarization flight with that helicopter as well as the the SE.3130 Alouette II manufactured by Sud (and later by Aérospatiale) that made use of a turbine engine, rather than a piston engine, and later went into widespread use with the European military services performing numerous roles including reconnaissance, aerial photographic, search and rescue (SAR), personnel transport, and anti-armor/maritime missions. The Alouette also saw service with civil authorities serving in med-evac., agricultural, and heavy lifter capacities. In 1963, the Alouette became the first commercially operated turbine helicopter in the U.S.

During the late 1950s and early 1960s, Jack conducted flight evaluations of a series of new helicopters that used the revolutionary hingeless rotor blade concept. This series of helicopters began with the Lockheed CL-475 in the late 1950s and the Bell H-13G during the early 1960s. Hingeless rotors with autostabilization systems provided greatly enhanced control power, maneuverability and stability while reducing maintenance and complexity by reducing blade hinges and mechanisms. During the early 1960s, several single-rotor and multirotor hingeless concepts were evaluated in Langley wind tunnels (Full Scale Tunnel and Transonic Dynamics Tunnel) and in flight.[12] Reeder flew The test rotorcraft for the flight studies, a Bell H-13G helicopter purchased by Langley from Bell, in 1962. In the official NASA report documenting the flight studies, Langley engineers Robert J. Huston and Robert J. Tapscott concluded: "A flight investigation of a nonarticulated rotor helicopter has demonstrated values of control power and damping an order of magnitude greater than have been obtained with conventional articulated rotors. The measured loads on the hingeless rotor, throughout the flight envelope of this investigation, were not above the design fatigue loads. However, the results indicate that compromises between maneuverability and center-of-gravity travel may be required to maintain an adequate life on dynamic components of the nonarticulated rotor. A much greater degree of understanding of the hingeless rotor system is still required before the fundamental knowledge needed for general application of the system is complete."[13]

Sikorsky S-62/5H-3A Sea King and Lockheed XH-51N

Hingeless rotorcraft designs quickly advanced with more capability, such as the Lockheed XH-51N and the XH-51N compound helicopters. The compound model featured a turbojet engine to permit higher-speed studies. Reeder and other Langley pilots performed flight research studies in these rotorcraft, with objectives of providing data for structural loads, performance analysis, and updating helicopter handling criteria. The powerful control capability of the XH-51 provided more areas of interest to be expanded, and Jack's piloting skills, comments and knowledge contributed to the success of the project. The XH-51 compound was a highly efficient design that established a new rotorcraft world speed record at 487 mph in June 1967.

Sikorsky SH-3A Sea King helicopter at NASA Langley in 1972.

NASA Langley Research Center

Jack demonstrating the capabilities of the Lockheed XH-51N to British aviation officials at the Royal Aircraft Establishment (RAE) in England in 1965. The helicopter was loaned to the RAE for 20 flight hours. Note the lineup of RAE fixed wing flight-test subjects as well as a V/STOL P.1127 Harrier jump-jet prototype (first on the left).

NASA Langley Research Center via Jack Reeder

By the early 1960's, conventional rotorcraft designs had evolved tremendously in complexity as typified by such designs as the Sikorsky S-62/ HH-52A Sea Guardian (later Sea King) used by the Navy, Marine Corps, and Coast Guard. The S-62, a turbine-driven rotorcraft, was approved by the FAA for civil use in 1960 and became the first rotorcraft to utilize a "boat-hull" type fuselage. Langley acquired an S-62 for flight studies during the 1960s and Jack performed the majority of the research flights. In December 1972, Langley acquired a specially equipped Sikorsky SH-3A helicopter complete with state-of-the-art TV displays and monitoring equipment designed to enhance safety, efficiency, and accuracy of rotorcraft approaches and landings.

Jack conducted an exhaustive evaluation of the use of TV displays for approach and landing in the SH-3A in December 1972. In these studies, the glide angle, the lateral track, the slowdown, the desired touchdown location, and the actual touchdown were all judged from the TV picture. Vertical tape instruments provided auxiliary speed and height information to aid in the final slowdown to hover, with the standard, low-gain Sikorsky attitude stabilization system engaged. During the early 1960s, Reeder flew the Sikorsky S-61R (CH-3C) "Jolly Green Giant" which was used extensively in the SAR role during the Vietnam War by the USAF, as well as the nation's first practical gunship helicopter, the Bell Sioux Scout, a prototype of the famous Cobra series that also saw combat duty during the Vietnam War. In 1963, Jack described his experience flying the Sioux Scout in a 30-minute familiarization flight at Langley. The details of his comments follow, indicative of the vast amount of information he had absorbed in the short flight:

> *"The 'Sioux Scout' is basically an H-13 or Model 47 helicopter with a supercharged Lycoming engine rated at 260 horsepower at 20,000 feet. The gross weight is 2850 pounds. The two pilots sit in tandem, the forward pilot being lower and having excellent visibility. The forward pilot can either control the aircraft by means of a three-axis side-arm controller with the right hand and a console-mounted collective pitch stick, or the swiveling chin-mounted turret with twin machine guns through ± 100 degrees of arc by means of a swiveling optical sighting system. The rear pilot has normal center stick control and pedals. Controls about the roll and pitch axis are hydraulically powered.*
>
> *The fuselage is covered and highly faired to reduce drag. At the rear of the fuselage*

are a fixed horizontal tail with trailing edge deflected upward and a high aspect ratio vertical fin. A small fixed wing is mounted at appreciable positive incidence at the top of the fuselage at the rotor hub position. This wing also doubles as a fuel tank. In level flight, the wing is said to support approximately 500 pounds at 100 mph and 800 pounds at 125 mph.

The aircraft seems to be 30 mph or more, faster than the H-13 for about the same engine manifold pressure settings. In cruise at 24 inches mp at 110 mph the vibration was mild and increased only slightly in turns up to about 40 degrees bank. At 125 mph indicated (actually 120 mph) the vibration had become strong but, again, it did not build up rapidly with normal acceleration in turns or pullups. In the turns at both 110 and 125 mph it was apparent that considerably steeper turns could be made without loss of either speed or altitude than could the standard H-13 or most other present-day helicopters, as a matter of fact. The longitudinal stability of the helicopter in the maneuver sense at 110 or 125 mph as determined in both pullups and turns was judged to be good. Thus, the characteristics described gave the aircraft a 'solid' feeling in longitudinal maneuvers at cruising and high speed that most present-day helicopters lack.

The static directional stability was found to be good and entries into turns at climb and cruise speeds could be made without the need for directional control application. Lateral-directional oscillation at about 100 mph damped in about 1-1/2 cycles following a pedal displace-and-return, and oscillations were not excited by the mild turbulence that existed. These characteristics were thought to be good.

There is a moderate but definite buildup in vibration when rolling into or out of turns with only a moderate rate of roll. This is similar to that experienced in the H-13. There seemed to be very little pitching due to rolling velocity with this aircraft, however, which is a desirable improvement over the H-13. The H-13 and others with gyro-devices in the control systems have exhibited nose-down pitching with right rolling and nose-up pitching with left rolling (all having the same direction of rotor rotation).

The wing has, I was told, increased the speed for best climb to about 60 mph, and the maximum rotor rpm in autorotation now occurs at 60–80 mph with a lower rpm at 120 mph. It was said that there was no problem in establishing autorotation from a throttle chop at 120 mph, however.

In hovering flight, the aircraft was steady and smooth at all angles to the wind, which was light. Control was adequate, but there were large changes in fuselage attitude for trim as hovering was established from forward flight, at varying angles to the wind in hover, and upon approaching the ground for a vertical landing. These trim changes are not necessarily different from those of other helicopters of the model 47 or H-13 type, though.

The side-arm controls at the forward station were certainly practical and easy to use, although coordinating yaw with roll, pitch, and, particularly, power does not come naturally to the conventionally trained pilot. Undesirable characteristics that should be corrected, however, are the magnitude of the 'breakout' forces about all axes of the three-axis control, and the lack of feel forces. The breakout force, although not limiting, should be reduced for easy and accurate use of the control, particularly in yaw. Also, I believe that light feel-force gradients would improve the controller, particularly in roll and pitch. I do not think it is necessary to provide exact centering with a feel spring arrangement, though. An added preload to achieve exact centering may well destroy what is gained by light gradients and the reduction of breakout forces that now exist.

In summary, this aircraft provides a smooth, steady gun platform up to 100–110 mph in light turbulence, and represents a considerable improvement over other articulated helicopters of this weight category. In addition, the aircraft has good longitudinal maneuvering capability with a 'solid' feel in maneuvering flight up to 110 mph at least, which is significantly better than other articulated helicopters of this category within my experience.

Also, the side-arm control arrangement is a very feasible system for controlling the aircraft comfortably and accurately and is very practical as it opens up the center of the cockpit for other equipment. It is felt that the 'quality' of the three-axis side-arm controller should be improved and a suitable 'feel' system developed for it."[15]

Other Rotocraft

Other important rotorcraft flown by Reeder included the Huey AH-1G Cobra, flown at Langley in studies to determine the aerodynamic behavior of main rotor blade airfoil sections and acoustical effects; the Sikorsky CH-54B Skycrane, which was tested for its heavy lifting capabilities at Langley in 1972; the Vertol 107 or CH-46C Sea Knight used at NASA Langley in 1972 to effectively demonstrate the first automatic vertical landing system for helicopters; and the highly successful CH-47 Chinook, flown at Langley in the VTOL Approach and Landing Technique (VALT) program to determine the feasibility of automated navigational

The Twirly Birds

In addition to being a member of the team that drafted the original military specifications for flying qualities of helicopters, Jack was a founding member of the Twirly Birds, an exclusive and elite International Organization of the pioneering pilots of helicopters and other vertical take-off aircraft founded in 1949. Founder members are individuals who soloed a helicopter or other vertical take-off aircraft in sustained complete flight, including a take-off and landing prior to V-J Day (14 August 1945).

Jack's expertise and experience with the world of vertical takeoff and landing helicopters would greatly complement his activities flying convertiplanes and V/STOL aircraft, as described in a later chapter. Perhaps former Langley engineer Robert Tapscott best summarized his legacy to the rotorcraft community: "He pioneered handling qualities criteria of helicopters, which was probably the most significant thing he contributed to the development of rotorcraft."[14]

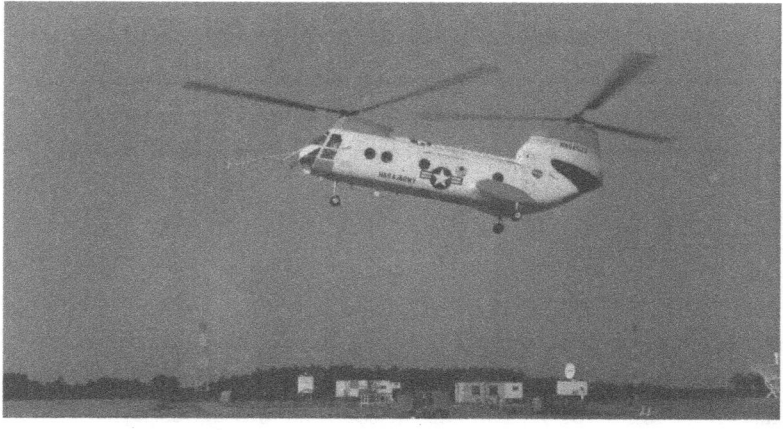

Boeing Vertol CH-46C Sea Knight at NASA Wallops Island, Virginia, in 1972.

NASA Langley Research Center

After Neil Armstrong's moon mission, he served as Deputy Associate Administrator for the NASA Office of Advanced Research and Technology (OART) at Headquarters. During a visit to Langley in 1970, he was briefed by Gerald Rainey (left) and Jack Reeder on a tilt-rotor wind-tunnel model slated for aeroelastic tests in the Langley Transonic Dynamics Tunnel.

NASA Langley Research Center

Group photo of participants and the Boeing Vertol CH-47 Chinook used in the highly successful NASA Langley VALT program. Jack Reeder can be seen kneeling in bottom row (fourth from right).

NASA Langley Research Center via Jack Reeder

Bell AH-1G Cobra gunship helicopter
NASA Langley Research Center

Langley engineers and pilots put the heavy lifting capability of the Sikorsky CH-54B Skycrane to the test. Here, a NASA CH-54B hovers into position to hoist a T-38 Talon jet trainer from the tarmac in 1973.

(NASA Langley Research Center via Larry Loftin)

Boeing Vertol CH-46C Sea Knight at NASA Wallops Island, Virginia, in 1972.

NASA Langley Research Center

Chapter 5 Notes

1. Wheatley, John B. and Hood, Manley J. (1936). <u>NACA Report 515: Full-Scale Wind Tunnel Tests of a PCA-2 Autogiro Rotor</u>. National Advisory Committee for Aeronautics, Langley Memorial Aeronautical Laboratory, Langley Field, Va.

2. Bailey, F.J., Jr. and Gustafson, F.B. (1939). <u>NACA TN-741: Observations in Flight of the Region of Stalled Flow over the Blades of an Autogiro Rotor</u>. National Advisory Committee for Aeronautics, Langley Memorial Aeronautical Laboratory, Langley Field, Va.

3. Dingeldein, Richard C. and Schaefer, Raymond F. (1948). <u>NACA Report 905: Full-Scale Investigation of Aerodynamic Characteristics of a Typical Single-Rotor Helicopter in Forward Flight</u>. NACA Langley Memorial Aeronautical Laboratory, Langley Field, Va.

4. Reeder, J. P. and Gustafson, F. B. (April 22, 1948). <u>Notes on the Flying Qualities of Helicopters</u>, Presented at the American Helicopter Society Meeting April 22–24, 1948. National Advisory Committee for Aeronautics, Washington and Langley Aeronautical Laboratory, Langley Field, Va., p. 1.

5. Ibid., pp. 2-4.

6. Ibid., p. 7.

7. NACA Langley Memorandum from Engineer-Test Pilot John P. Reeder to Chief of Flight Research Division (January 26, 1948). "Flight in Bendix Model K helicopter". Langley Field, Va., pp. 1-2.

8. Reeder, J. P. and Whitten, J. B. (September 26, 1951). <u>NACA Technical Note 2459: Some Effects of Varying the Damping in Pitch and Roll on the Flying Qualities of a Small Single-Rotor Helicopter</u>. National Advisory Committee for Aeronautics, Langley Aeronautical Laboratory, Langley Field, Va., p. 1.

9. Reeder, J. P. (October 26, 1954). <u>NACA: Notes on Helicopter Flight Research</u>. National Advisory Committee for Aeronautics, Langley Aeronautical Laboratory, Langley Field, Va., p. 1.

10. Ibid, pp. 5, 6, 8.

11. Ibid, p. 14.

12. Ward, J.F. (January 1, 1965). <u>NASA-TM-X-56726, 19650101: A Summary of Hingeless-Rotor Structural Loads and Dynamics Research</u>. National Aeronautics and Space Administration, NASA Langley Research Center, Hampton, Va.

13. Huston, Robert J. and Tapscott, Robert J. (December 10–12, 1962). <u>The Results of Some Wind Tunnel and Flight Studies with Helicopters at NASA</u>, To be Presented at New York Academy of Sciences Conference on Vertical Take-Off and Landing Aircraft, New York, N.Y. NASA Langley Research Center, Langley Station, Hampton, Va., p. 14.

14. NASA Langley Research Center Memorandum to 249/Flight Research Branch, Low-Speed Aircraft Division (Attn: Gene C. Moen) from 246A/Chief, Research Aircraft Flight Division (January 10, 1973). "Evaluation of TV Display System in SH-3A Helicopter". NASA Langley Research Center, Hampton, Va., pp. 1-2.

15. NASA Langley Memorandum for Associate Director from John P. Reeder, Assistant Chief Flight Mechanics and Technology Division (December 31, 1963). "Flight report on Bell 'Sioux Scout' helicopter". NASA Langley Research Center, Hampton, Va., pp. 1-3.

16. Reeder, John P. (unpublished material dated June 1973). "Notes on AH-1G, Two Flights of 0.3 and 0.5 Hours, Respectively". NASA Langley Research Center, Hampton, Va., pp. 1-2.

17. Interview with Robert Tapscott. (March 29, 2006). Yorktown, Va.

Chapter Six
Big Guys and Little Guys

The Lockheed XC-35 served as NACA/NASA Langley's first "storm-chaser" aircraft. The aircraft is outfitted with a rain collector boom mounted under the nose.

NASA Langley Research Center

Above: Jack prepares for a flight in the Douglas C-54D Skymaster.

NASA Langley Research Center via Larry Loftin

Below: Jack landing a Douglas C-54D Skymaster at Langley following the successful completion of a research flight.

NASA Langley Research Center via Jack Reeder

In addition to flight testing high-performance fighters, bombers, and rotorcraft, Jack Reeder's activities included research projects involving military and civil transports, as well as civil general aviation airplanes. His research flying hours in transport aircraft began in 1943 with programs involving the revolutionary Lockheed XC-35, which was designed for the Army for high-altitude research.

Lockheed XC-35 in flight.

United States Air Force

The aircraft also held the distinction of being NACA/NASA Langley's first "storm-chaser" aircraft, with Herb Hoover performing the majority of research flights into severe thunderstorms. This pioneering work would later be followed in the 1970s and 1980s at Langley with flights of an F-106B and other aircraft. The aircraft was also used to perform flight studies on the formation of aircraft contrails and how to reduce their visibility, important factors that would benefit American high-altitude heavy bomber crews flying in the skies over Europe during World War II. The aircraft was later modified and equipped with turbo-supercharged engines for high-altitude research flights, with Reeder performing the majority of these flights.

Liasion Aircraft

Throughout the 1940s and 1950s, Jack flew an NACA Lockheed 12 liaison aircraft used to transport engineers and technical staff members to

Mel Gough handles the central vertical fin of the NACA Lockheed 12 liaison aircraft.

NASA Langley Research Center

NACA Headquarters and other NACA facilities or business destinations. For enhanced stability and aircraft performance, a central vertical fin was incorporated in the tail assembly. In addition, Reeder and other Langley research pilots flew a Douglas C-47 in a liaison role at Langley that continued from 1946 until 1971, when it was reassigned to the NASA Lewis Research Center. Reeder also flew a Douglas R4D, the Navy's version of the C-47, for several years at Langley. In 1946, Jack performed flight tests to investigate the effects of friction in the controls of a Douglas C-54D Skymaster transport. His assessment was summarized in an official NACA Research Memorandum documenting the studies: "During the handling-qualities tests of a C-54D airplane, it was found that the friction in the control system was about double the limits of the Army and Navy requirements for stability and control. The friction was reduced to about one-half of the Army-Navy limits by removing the automatic-pilot servo units, and this investigation was conducted to determine the effects of reducing the friction.

Navy Beech C-45 transport used by NACA Langley to study the concept of alleviating wind gusts encountered by aircraft in flight. Note the special gust sensor on the nose boom of the airplane.

NASA Langley Research Center

Time histories of normal landings and of attempts to bracket the edges of a radio beam are presented both with the servo-units in and out. Examination and comparison of the time histories with high and low friction reveals that friction was particularly troublesome in precision flying involving small control displacements because with high friction control movement did not necessarily follow all force applications. The comparison also shows that the friction requires excessive physical exertion on the part of the pilot. The control system with approximately double the friction allowed by the Army-Navy requirements was unsatisfactory for precision flying, whereas the control system with approximately one-half the specified friction was satisfactory."[1] Blind landing approaches were also studied in the Skymaster.

Navy Beech C-45

Jack's ceaseless attention to safety issues were quite evident during another "close call" he experienced while flying a military twin-engine propeller-driven transport over Utah during the 1950's. He recalled years later:

"In the 1950s, I went to Ogden AFB (about 5000 feet above sea level) to take delivery on a Beech C-45(D-18) from the Depot there. After preliminaries, I, my chief of maintenance, and the crew chief from Ogden took off with full fuel for an acceptance flight. After takeoff at about 300 feet above the runway the left engine failed with a bang and some smoke. I shut the engine down, cleaned up the airplane, maintained a straight course with full power on the right engine at best climb speed and noted about a 100 feet-per-minute climb. The propellers were of the non-feathering type so the left propeller control had been placed in low rpm position. I declared an emergency. My first thought was to head for Ogden Municipal in the valley ahead, but to my dismay snow showers had obliterated visibility in the valley. I had to turn back. In the turn I could not prevent loss of altitude. A waiting airplane blocked the most suitable runway. Finally, when still descending slowly and at about 100 feet, I decided I had to turn into the field, aiming for the intersection of the two main runways and bisecting the angle between them. I turned the airplane as rapidly as possible to conserve altitude, entering buffeting as I did so, and rolled out with a bare margin in speed. I then saw wires across my path on the upsloping terrain to the runways. There was no way to go over them without stalling. I put the nose down and fitted the airplane under the wires and between the poles. I came out a few feet above the ground and held the aircraft in ground effect. I gained speed as I climbed along the upslope for about 3000 feet to the runway intersection. I then pulled up, put wheels and landing flaps down, turned onto the runway and made a normal landing. The operations officer didn't believe the story about the wires, so we went out in a staff car to show them to him. The wires were about 20 feet off the ground and, because of the sloping terrain, they couldn't be seen from the ground or tower at operations. Actually, for a few moments, operations thought we

had crashed.'[2]

During the mid to late 1950s, Langley engineers W. Hewitt Phillips and Christopher Kraft Jr. focused their expertise on providing concepts for alleviating the effects of wind gusts encountered by aircraft in flight. To study the problem more extensively, a Navy Beech C-45 transport aircraft that had been previously acquired by Langley in 1949 was modified to accommodate a special gust sensor housed in the nose of the airplane

NACA Grumman J4F Widgeons with hull modification shown on aircraft on the left.

NASA Langley Research Center via Larry Loftin

and controlled the wing flaps by means of a special hydraulic system. Jack performed several test flights in this aircraft, effectively demonstrating the gust alleviation system devised by Phillips and Kraft.

Grumman J4F Widgeons

In 1948, Langley acquired several versions of the Grumman J4F Widgeon utility flying boat and Grumman JRF-5 utility flying boat that were flown by Reeder and other Langley research pilots to NACA/NASA Wallops Island, Va. and other business destinations. The NACA also investigated the performance of various hull designs on these aircraft. Following the transition of the NACA to NASA in October 1958, Langley acquired a Convair T-29 from the Air Force. The T-29, another version of the Convair 240 airliner, was flown by Langley pilots as a liaison aircraft for the agency's administrator.

While the aircraft did not possess the best aerodynamic performance characteristics, NASA operated it in an administrative liaison role until 1963. NASA then obtained a Grumman as a replacement for this aircraft, which was also flown by Reeder and other NASA research pilots, performing efficiently in the liaison role for the agency. NASA also used the Gulfstream to help research pilots maintain their piloting proficiencies, particularly under instrument operations. Larry Loftin observed,

> *"These pilots might be on call 24 hours a day for 7 days a week, and accordingly received a significant amount of overtime pay for extra duty and duty outside the normal working day. Although not overtly expressed, these monetary factors may have influenced some pilots' opinions. The other group of pilots felt that the transport operation made serious inroads on the time available for the pilot to fulfill his primary responsibility which was research flying and associated analysis of data and the study and writing of technical papers. Reeder was in this latter group, and felt strongly that the requirements for operation of the Administrator's aircraft on a standby basis, including required rest periods from flying, was preventing the newer pilots from learning their jobs as research pilots. Finally, in the mid-1970's, flying of the Gulfstream at Langley as well as those aircraft on administrative duties at other Centers was put on contract, which ended the controversy. Maintenance of all NASA Gulfstream aircraft had been carried out under contract."[8]*

During the 1950's, Reeder flew the Lockheed Electra turboprop airliner that later evolved into the highly successful Lockheed P-3 Orion Anti-Submarine Warfare aircraft for the Navy. Both aircraft designs benefited from the pioneering supersonic propeller engine technology tests flown by Reeder at Langley on the XF-88B supersonic propeller research test bed (covered in Chapter 4). In 1972, Jack flew a DeHavilland DHC-6 Twin Otter short takeoff and landing (STOL) commuter liner that was later modified for lightning flight research studies conducted at Langley in 1978, becoming Langley's second storm-chaser research aircraft.

Boeing 367-80B (Dash 80)

Jack's experience flying large commercial jet transports began in 1965 when he had the opportunity to perform a series of simulation and flight research studies in the Boeing 367-80B (also known as the "Dash 80"), prototype of the famous 707 jetliner, which became the first large modern commercial airliner to enter service with international airlines. In 1955, the Dash 80 broke new ground when it established a new non-stop transcontinental record, flying from coast to coast in just over 8 hours.

Boeing 367-80B performing low-speed flight with blown flaps deployed.

NASA Langley Research Center

The Dash 80 was the first large commercial jet to serve as a flying research airplane at Langley. Jack, along with other Langley research pilots, assessed short takeoff and landing methods in the Dash 80, which had been modified to include blown flaps that significantly increased lift at low speeds. The fundamental flying quality assessments that came from this early work, augmented with other simulator and flight tests at Langley and Ames, provided the basis for the design of the highly successful Boeing C-17 Globemaster. The first NASA noise-reduction studies for large commercial transports were also conducted at Langley using the Dash 80 aircraft. In addition, the nation's first supersonic transport (SST) in-flight simulation studies were performed in the Dash 80, which produced a wealth of knowledge, data, and lessons learned that were incorporated in the first U.S. SST Program in the 1960s and 1970s.

During the late 1950's Reeder flew familiarization and evaluation flights in the Douglas DC-8 jetliner, another modern jetliner that served in the commercial airline industry until 1999. By 1973, Reeder had also acquired experience flying the Boeing 727 and 737 jetliners. Then, in 1973, he made the trip to Seattle to fly the new 747 jumbo jet at Boeing's aircraft plant. Jack's comments on the characteristics of the 747 were:

The Dash 80 configured for SST simulation studies at NASA Langley during the 1960s.

NASA Langley Research Center

"I had a chance to fly the Boeing 747 test airplane during a flight-test operation to certify the GE CF-6 engines for proper cooling under various operating conditions. One engine, number 3, was instrumented. An FAA test pilot did most of the flying from the pilot's seat. Ray McPherson, senior Boeing test pilot, acted as co-pilot for the FAA pilot and myself. The whole operation required about 8 ¾ hours, including the

pre-flight briefing. About 5 hours were spent in the air.

The take-off thrust available was nominally about 51,000 lbs./engine. During climb tests, the aircraft reached a service ceiling (about 100 fpm rate of climb) at 43,000' pressure altitude (45,000' had been planned) with maximum climb thrust. After leveling off the Mach number climbed to an indicated 0.822 at this thrust. Descent was made to 41,000' where a Mach number of 0.845 was held with maximum cruise thrust.

The aircraft was not equipped with control wheel steering or autoland. It did have an autopilot and a single inertial navigation and guidance system. After initial tests were completed, I took control of the aircraft from the left front seat for 1 hour and 10 minutes of flying. From about 75 miles out, I executed a descent from 15,000 ft, instrument approach maneuvers, landing and taxi to the ramp for shutdown at Moses Lake. After ground tests with number 3 engine for about 1 ½ hours, all engines were started and I taxied out, took off, climbed to 15,000' and established a steady cruise of 200K for engine test purposes. I flew IFR to Seattle (124 n.mi.) and executed an idle power descent to 2,000' at which time I was relieved by the FAA pilot for checks of aircraft controllability down to 160K with controls powered by two windmilling engines (2 inboards windmilling, 2 outboards in idle with hydraulic pumps shut off).

Control forces, which I was flying, were estimated by MacPherson to be 65 lbs./g at 250–300K, 15–20 lbs. for full lateral control, and 60 lbs. for full rudder throw. The longitudinal force with deflection was not stated but from ground checks I would guess the force at maximum throw to be about 40 lbs. All force gradients seemed linear. Friction breakout forces were estimated at 5 lbs. for, 7 lbs. for longitudinal control, and 15 lbs. for the rudder. I flew the aircraft only in a manual mode. The response to aileron deflection in terms of angular acceleration and rolling velocity seemed linear with deflection and was considered satisfactorily high (Cooper Rating of 2) for the moderate deflections explored. No lag in the development of response was apparent, and no roll overshoot was evident upon centering the wheel. The aileron control forces were suitable for comfortable one hand operation in normal maneuvering, approach and landing. The friction present, although I would prefer it lower, did not interfere with precision control nor make wheel centering or trimming difficult. A roll-yaw interconnect (rudder applied with roll input) was provided to minimize adverse yaw with rolling. An apparent residual adverse sideslip was evidenced by the presence of a sideforce but was not objectionable for normal wheel inputs (no pilot inputs to rudder). With quick roll inputs the automatic rudder inputs excited an undesirable lateral fuselage vibration at the cockpit. In summary, roll control was satisfactorily powerful and precise with no tendency for over control. With regard to over control, this aircraft is a 'dream' compared with some other transports which have roll control characteristics which tend to drive the pilot toward a high frequency lateral PIO (pilot induced oscillation) during the landing approach. This PIO tendency is not simply a sensitivity due to size and control power since modern, high-performance fighters and executive jets do not exhibit such tendencies in roll. Hence, I was curious as to whether the tendency would be present in the larger 747 aircraft.

The longitudinal maneuvering force in turns at constant speed was suitable for one hand operation although I would prefer it lighter. The rudder forces and deflections were well harmonized with the ailerons, and the rudder forces were pleasantly light, but not too light. The rudder was easy to use accurately for turn coordination or yaw control. Use of speed brakes (wing spoilers) in the clean configuration for speed and descent control resulted in progressively increasing buffeting with deflection, as felt in the cockpit. Mild buffet was all that was experienced for the spoiler required in my maneuvers. Little or no trim change was experienced with spoiler deflection, a very desirable characteristic. Longitudinal trim changes with gear and flap operation were pleasantly low and readily handled with one hand. The longitudinal trim change with thrust, nose up with increased thrust, was undesirably large and the effects immediately apparent when controlling glide path and speed on approach. This characteristic tended to offset corrections to speed or to cause speed deviations during corrections to glide path. Corrections could be made readily with one hand because of the desirably light longitudinal control force gradient with deflection, but too much attention had to be devoted to speed control.

The approach and landing at Moses Lake (Grant County Airport) was made with a light wind quartering from the tail. Little turbulence was evident. The aircraft was easy to maneuver laterally on the approach and easy to keep aligned with the runway. I was told to hold a speed of 1.3 V_p plus 10 knots because of low engine thrust response (and trim change with thrust, as I found out). A desired change in thrust seemed to require about 3 seconds at approach power. It was clear that anticipation and lead time were required in thrust adjustments. Except for the attention that had to be paid to speed control, no difficulty was experienced in tracking the glide slope of the ILS.

The landing flare maneuver was initiated at a radio altimeter height of 50'. With this cue as a start, the flare was surprisingly easy to judge. Longitudinal control was very positive with good control power, good aircraft stability and damping, and pleasantly light forces. The hold off to a low speed, nose high landing with thrust reduced to idle during round out was easily accomplished with one hand. Lowering the nose wheel was easily and gently controlled all the way to contact. Inertially derived speed was used for ground operation because of difficulty in judging speed from the high cockpit elevation. We seemed to be moving very slowly when the inertial speed was 45K and I was cautioned to slow to 15–18K for a right angle turn to prevent excessive tire scrubbing (the inboard main trucks steer with the nose gear when operated by the tiller; the rudder pedals steer only the nose gear).

Rotation for the takeoff was very easily accomplished with one hand. The aircraft showed no hesitation at the start of rotation and no tendency to pitch up at lift off. The attitude could be precisely controlled with easy one-hand forces and an 18° deck angle second segment (take off flaps and safety speed plus 10K) climb out was made followed by noise abatement schedules for flaps, speed and thrust. Precise speed, altitude and laterally level flight were easily set up and trimmed for cruise at 220K at 15,000' for engine test purposes on the way back to Seattle. A portion of this leg of the flight was in cloud.

All-in-all, the aircraft was an easy, precise, docile aircraft to fly, considering its size. Flying qualities were very good (Cooper Rating 2) overall for the range of operation covered. The one detracting quality was the nose up trim change with increased thrust (and vice versa), particularly considering the approach."[34]

The Concorde

During the early 1980s, Jack had the opportunity to test fly the Concorde, achieving a cruising speed of Mach 2 during his test flight.

British Airways Corporation via Larry Loftin

During the latter 1960's, Reeder was invited to test fly Lockheed's L-1011-500 Tri Star wide body commercial airliner, and during the early 1980s, he had the opportunity to test fly the Concorde, achieving a cruising speed of Mach 2 during his test flight. Jack was very excited over his Concorde flight, and bent the ear of many Langley staff members regarding the event. He was especially impressed by the noticeable expansion of the fuselage at Mach 2 due to heating.

Jack's experiences with flying general aviation (GA) aircraft, which had begun prior to his flight research career at Langley, continued throughout his career as a research pilot with NACA/NASA Langley. For example, during the 1940s, he sharpened his piloting skills flying such aircraft as the SR-8E, a classic aircraft design of the Golden Era of aviation that utilized supercharger technology and gull wings for high-altitude flights.

Stinson Sentinel Aircraft

Stinson L-5E Sentinel Aircraft used in Langley noise reduction research. Note five-bladed propeller and muffler.

NASA Langley Research Center

Jack was involved in one of the more unique flight research projects involving general aviation aircraft at Langley, flight testing a highly modified Stinson L-5E Sentinel during 1946 in airplane noise-reduction research studies. The NACA had initiated a major program to reduce the noise of personal-owner aircraft in the area around airports. In addition to theoretical and ground-based studies, a flight experiment was conducted.

The L-5E was modified with a five-blade propeller, geared-down engine, special muffler (designed by the staff of the Full Scale Tunnel) for reduced noise operations. The "quiet" airplane had been demonstrated at the Sixteenth Annual Inspection of Langley, attended by representatives of the aeronautical community. The results of the demonstration were remarkable, with many in attendance awed at the low noise level of a direct overflight. For example, the unmodified airplane had to fly at an altitude of 1600 ft. to reduce its noise levels to those exhibited by the modified airplane during a 200-ft flyover. Unfortunately, the weight of the muffler system and other factors made application to personal aircraft unfeasible, but a striking example of a quiet airplane had made an indelible impression on designers and regulators.[5]

In 1950, Jack participated in flight studies of a specially instrumented Beech 35 four-seat Bonanza aircraft with an objective of measuring the flying qualities of a high-performance personal-owner airplane to investigate the possible causes of instrument flying accidents with aircraft of that general type. Reeder, researcher James J. Adams and fellow test pilot James B. Whitten performed these studies. In their summary report, the team concluded:

> *"The results of the investigation show that the test airplane satisfactorily meets most present-day flying qualities requirements. It was found, however, that the lateral oscillations were marginally damped and that there was no aerodynamic warning prior to the stall, which is characterized by a rapid roll-off. The airplane was subject to continuous lateral oscillations in rough air, and these lateral oscillations continually excited the rate-of-turn indicator. Since the pilot depends on the rate-of-turn indicator to show changes in airplane attitude when there is no directional gyro or artificial horizon, this characteristic made instrument flying more difficult. Other factors, which might affect the instrument flying qualities, are the rapid spiral divergence at low speed and the ease with which the airplane can exceed its maximum allowable airspeed in relatively*

> *gradual dives. It was found that, during simulated instrument conditions, recoveries from unusual attitudes could be made with little control movement, and without the airplane exceeding its airspeed and acceleration limits.*
>
> *The lack of aerodynamic stall warning and the rapid roll-off at the stall could contribute to stall-spin accidents with high-performance personal-owner aircraft. In a take-off, accidents could be caused by the fact that the airplane could be pitched to an angle of attack beyond the stall where sufficient power to climb was not available."*[6]

During his career at Langley, Reeder was able to test fly most of the production U.S. general aviation aircraft, and he also participated in evaluations of experimental aircraft such as a Cessna L-19 which had been modified by Mississippi State University with suction boundary layer control (BLC) incorporated into the wing design for enhanced Short Takeoff and Landing (STOL) performance.[7] Reeder's other GA experiences included test flying the Mooney 21, equipped with wing leveler mechanisms designed to alleviate spiral instability, which had proven to be a major factor in loss of control and orientation in adverse weather IFR conditions. Jack also flew the modified American Yankee AA-1 in the latter 1960s and 1970s, which was flown primarily by Langley rest pilot James Patton in the Langley Stall/Spin Program for GA aircraft. During that program, Langley pilots successfully deployed an emergency spin recovery parachute on the airplane 28 times to successfully terminate spins. Jim Patton received national recognition for his role as chief pilot in the program when he received the Iven C. Kincheloe Award of the Society of Experimental Test Pilots in 1978. Reeder also successfully test flew the Piper Cherokee Arrow PA-28R T-tail configured GA aircraft that was also used for research in the program.

Rutan "Defiant" Twin-Engine GA Aircraft

Toward the end of his career at NASA Langley, Reeder had the opportunity to perform an evaluation flight in an unconventional GA prototype aircraft design. The Rutan "Defiant", designed by the famous Burt Rutan, featured a unique canard, a swept wing with winglets, and tractor/pusher propellers. Rutan's objectives in designing the Defiant was to provide an inherently stall-resistant airplane with safe engine-out handling qualities.

Rutan "Defiant" twin-engine GA aircraft at Langley.
NASA Langley Research Center

Reeder later described his impressions of flying the aircraft:

> "The 'Defiant' prototype, N78RA, is a 4-place light-twin aircraft having a 'loaded canard' configuration of unusual construction. It combines safe flight features with high performance and long range. The rudder surface projects downward under the left side of the fuselage nose and can be operated (in this prototype) only by the pilot on the left. Roll and pitch control is achieved through side-arm control sticks at the forward end of arm-rests on the cabin walls, on the left side for the pilot and on the right side for the co-pilot.
>
> The designers and builders, the Rutan Brothers, Burt and Dick, flew the aircraft to Langley for a two-day visit on December 11 and 12, 1978. I had the opportunity to observe and evaluate the aircraft briefly from the right front seat (no rudder pedals) with Dick Rutan as pilot. The aircraft had about half fuel and no baggage at take off.
>
> The aircraft is a result of much innovative and logical thinking. It has very good performance and engine-out safety design features. Roll control effectiveness is not adequate and both roll and longitudinal control forces (including friction) are too high, all of which are scheduled for improvement. Longitudinal and lateral-directional stability are

satisfactory except for the tendency for large roll upsets due to gusts below cruise speed."[8]

In 1982, Jack recounted his first flight experience in his personal GA aircraft, a restored Monocoupe that he acquired in 1972:

"On my first flight in my current Monocoupe 90AL-125 in 1972, the engine stopped for good while I was slowing to check stalling speed. I was northwest of Williamsburg and had the airport in sight, but quickly determined that I couldn't reach it. Several farms below had standing water on them and the furrows were at 90 degrees to the wind. I quickly picked the only satisfactory looking field as it was passing by, although it was small (about 1000 feet across). It was bounded by a road on one side, a woods and a fence on my planned approach site. A 270-degree turn was required. On the far end there was a house with garden and garage to its rear, which placed them across my landing path. A steep gulley lay to my right. I assumed a glide speed of about 65 mph by feel as I had not had a chance to stall the aircraft. I turned over the road, side slipped through a gap in the trees and over the fence, landed in tall grass headed for the garden diagonally across the field. I found the braking moderately effective and rolled to a stop short of the garage with corn stalks under my left wing. There was no damage.

A preacher lived in the house and arrived home just after I landed, but had not known of the airplane in his yard until I knocked on his door. The driver of a truck had seen my landing and had come back to help. He took me back to Newport News for a mechanic. Without finding the cause of the engine stoppage, the engine ran normally several hours later. The preacher, who volunteered his help, came home immediately after church the next day, Sunday, and mowed a 750-foot runway for my takeoff. While the runway was being mowed the old gentleman who owned the field took me around the country neighborhood in his Lincoln to meet the local folks. Later, the preacher and his family stood waving as I took off.

Before I learned the cause of my engine stoppage it occurred several times again during landing, after which the engine couldn't be started for two hours or more. It turned out that the magnetos were old and had not been replaced at overhaul. The coils were breaking down under heat-soak conditions and would not provide a spark."[9]

Jack Reeder's GA flight-testing experience also included flying three business jet designs that figured prominently in the business jet market. These included the Lockheed Jetstar in the 1960s and 1970s, the Lear Jet 23 in 1960, and the Grumman Gulfstream II in 1965.

NASA Langley research pilots pose for a photo beside Langley's new Gulfstream I in front of the NASA Langley flight research hangar in 1963. Langley research pilots Bill Alford (second from left), Jack Reeder (fourth from left), Jim Whitten (fifth from left), Lee Person (sixth from left), and Robert "Bob" Champine (seventh from left) are shown in the photo.

NASA Langley Research Center

Grumman representative delivering a Gulfstream I to NASA Langley in 1963. Jack Reeder (left) accepted the delivery for NASA.

NASA Langley Research Center via Jack Reeder

Jack Reeder was an extremely active member of the U.S. aeronautics community. Here, Jack is caught off guard by the camera at a dinner of the Flight Safety Foundation, flanked by his friends John Stack (second from right) and George Bates (right).

(ack Reeder

Famous aviation personality Al Williams visited Langley for a tour in the early 1950s. Vice President of Aviation for the Gulf Oil Company, Williams was an air racer (winner of the Pulitzer Trophy and Schneider Cup), the former chief test pilot for the U.S. Navy, and an expert aerobatic pilot. He was one of the first to master the art of dive-bombing and demonstrated the technique internationally. His famous Gulfhawk biplane (a civilian version of the Grumman F3F Navy fighter) did much to popularize aviation in the 1930s. In the picture, he is joined by Jack Reeder (third from left) and Langley pilots Jim Whitten (second from right) and Bob Champine (right).

NASA Langley Research Center via Larry Loftin

Chapter Six Notes

1. Talmage, Donald B. and Reeder, John P. (November 8, 1948). <u>NACA Research Memorandum (RM No. L8G30a): The Effects of Friction in the Control System on the Handling Qualities of a C-54D Airplane.</u> National Advisory Committee for Aeronautics, Washington D.C. Langley Aeronautical Laboratory, Langley Field, Va., p. 1.

2. Reeder, John P. (Jack) (July 1, 1982). "Candidate Anecdotes". Part of NASA Langley Research Center Archives Collection, NASA Langley Research Center, Hampton, Va., pp. 3-4.

3. Loftin, Laurence K., Jr. (Unpublished Manuscript, July 1986). A Research Pilot's World as Seen from the Cockpit of a NASA Engineer-Pilot, Chap. 4, p. 8.

4. Reeder, John P. (September 17, 1973). <u>Boeing 747 Flight</u>.

5. Vogeley, A. W. (1948). NACA TN 1647: <u>Sound-level Measurements of a Light Airplane Modified to Reduce Noise Reaching the Ground.</u> National Advisory Committee for Aeronautics, Langley Aeronautical Laboratory, Hampton, Va.

6. Adams, James J. and Whitten, James B. <u>NACA Research Memorandum for the Civil Aeronautics Administration: Flying Qualities of a High-Performance Personal-Owner Airplane.</u> National Advisory Committee for Aeronautics, Washington D.C., Langley Aeronautical Laboratory, Langley Field, Va., p. 1.

7. Bridges, David H. Of Aeronautics, Aerophysics, and Aerospace: A History of Aerospace Engineering at Mississippi State University. <u>http://www.ae.msstate.edu/pages/bridges.php</u>

8. Reeder, John P. (December 12, 1978). "Observations from Flight in the Rutan 'Defiant' Prototype Aircraft". NASA, Langley Research Center, Hampton, Va., pp. 1 and 4.

9. Reeder, John P. (Jack) (July 1, 1982). "Candidate Anecdotes". Part of NASA Langley Research Center Archives, NASA Langley Research Center, Hampton, Va., pp. 4–5.

Chapter Seven
The V/STOL Challenge

Jack leaving the P.1127 after performing a successful test flight.

NASA Langley Research Center via Jack Reeder

Jack Reeder (right) during flight evaluations of the Bell X-14 aircraft at NASA Ames. Ames test pilot Fred Drinkwater (second from left) is also in the photo.

NASA Langley Research Center via Jack Reeder

Although the revolutionary mission capabilities of helicopters generated an unprecedented surge of applications within the civil and military communities, the limitations of rotorcraft (particularly speed) were widely recognized. While helicopters provided a hovering and load-lifting potential, many international efforts began to marry the flexibility and speed of conventional fixed-wing aircraft with the low-speed and vertical/short-take-off-and-landing (V/STOL) features of rotorcraft. During the late 1950s, 1960s, and early 1970s, a massive amount of research and development was undertaken on a world-wide basis on a multitude of different V/STOL concepts. Military interests were driven by an objective of achieving operations into unprepared, remotely dispersed landing sites and independence from conventional fixed airfields that could be obliterated by enemy strikes. Meanwhile, civil interests in V/STOL focused on the potential of commercial air transport operations into small airports with runway lengths far shorter than those required for normal air carrier aircraft. In attempting to achieve their goals, designers faced fundamental challenges common to all V/STOL concepts. These issues included excess power requirements, payload capacity, stability, controllability, and propulsion-induced problems such as performance reduction due to hot-gas ingestion, and erosion of landing sites from high velocity exhaust gases. Additional problems related to complexity, flying qualities (especially in cross winds), and engine-out characteristics also had to be resolved.

At Langley, innovative researchers formulated an impressive program on V/STOL that included analytical studies, wind-tunnel tests of powered models, and flight tests of NASA research aircraft and other test beds. In addition to extensive interactions with the U.S. industry and military, the Langley staff conducted several cooperative programs with foreign partners, especially those within the North Atlantic Treaty Organization (NATO). Special studies were jointly undertaken with British and German associates.

Jack Reeder had amassed a remarkable level of knowledge during his leadership in rotorcraft research and the development of helicopter flying quality requirements. His expertise was a vital ingredient in Langley's V/STOL research team.

Jack became one of the leading proponents of V/STOL flight, joining other famous Langley V/STOL pioneers, such as John P. Campbell, Richard E. Kuhn, Marion O. McKinney, and Robert H. Kirby, to form one of the world's most impressive and knowledgeable V/STOL technology teams. In fact, many senior Langley managers referred to this group as "The V/STOL Mafia" in view of their impressive credentials and ability to plan and conduct high-impact studies. Recognized on an international level for their expertise, these individuals were widely sought for their assessment of emerging V/STOL airplane concepts during the conceptual or developmental stage.

Jack's opinions and assessments of flying qualities were particularly in demand, and his career took off on a new, exciting path with a broad scope of V/STOL machines. He typically had the opportunity and distinction of serving as the lead NACA/NASA test pilot for several of these programs. A brief review of Jack's contributions follows, organized according to the type of propulsion system used by the various V/STOL machines he flew.

Short SC-1

One of the earliest types of V/STOL concepts was the lift-engine propulsive scheme, which used separate engines for vertical and cruise flight. In July 1962, Langley sent Jack to Bedford,

England to evaluate and assess the characteristics of the Short SC-1 airplane, which had been developed as a test bed to develop vertical-lift engines during the latter 1950s. Reeder described in detail his experiences flying the SC-1 in a Langley report in November 1966.

The Short SC-1 test bed hovering over a special platform.

Short via AIAA

Once again, major points of his evaluation are included to demonstrate the thorough engineering nature of Jack's flight-test assessments:

> *"The Short SC-1 aircraft is a delta-winged VTOL research aircraft using the lift-engine concept. The aircraft has a maximum off weight of 8,000 lbs., but for our*

hovering flights the take-off weight was somewhat less than 7,400 lbs. The aircraft has a bank of four lift engines and one propulsion engine, all of them being Rolls Royce RB-108s. These engines are designed as lift engines and have a thrust-to-weight ratio of 8:1 in hovering. The bank of lift engines is designed to be tilted 20 degrees aft of the hover position for acceleration and 15 degrees forward of hover for deceleration. The hover position is 3 degrees aft of the perpendicular to the wing chord.

The aircraft has normal airplane surface controls for airplane flight. For hover control, air is bled from the lift engines and exhausted through variable nozzles at the wing tips and the nose and tail. The system provides continuous and constant total bleed, which contributes to the lift. However, the nozzles are opened or closed differentially from their neutral positions to provide pitch and roll control. The yaw control is achieved by swiveling the pitch nozzles differentially in the lateral direction.

In this aircraft, the rudder and yaw displacement of the nozzles were controlled manually. The aileron surfaces were also manually operated. The elevator and the roll and pitch nozzles were powered hydraulically. However, the roll and pitch nozzles only were operated through the auto-stabilizer system such that they could respond to stabilization input signals.

The aircraft was extremely complex. The basic aircraft systems were each reasonably simple in principle, but the number of combinations in which the flight controls could be connected, and the number of handles, switches and warning lights in the cockpit was excessive. Furthermore, they were not arranged logically. After strapping into the cockpit it took 17 to 19 minutes to start the engines, and check the aircraft and stabilization systems up to the point of take off.

Engine starts and take-offs were accomplished over a special pit on the ground or on a special raised platform that took the lift-engine exhaust and ejected it away from the aircraft. This prevented the overheating of the ground surface, tires, brakes, and metal aircraft structure. Also, it eliminated the 15-percent suck down force that occurs over solid surfaces.

Flights all began with vertical take offs from the pit or platform. The take offs were made with brakes on, and maximum power was applied fairly quickly so as to rise rapidly to 20 or 30 feet, thus ensuring that the aircraft would not stray from the opening of the pit or platform before rising above the ground recirculation or interference region. The take off could be made from the platform or pit with enough fuel for 5- to 8-minute flights, depending on thrust required. In hover, the fuel consumption was about 160 lb./min. Evaluations were performed in hovering flight, and at speeds up to 90 knots over the runway at maximum heights of 50 to 75 feet. Lift engines were on at all times. Complete conversions to airplane flight were not made because the air inlet doors for the lift engines had been damaged in flight and had to be locked in the open position.

The three modes of operation of the auto-stabilization system were evaluated. In the rate-auto mode an intermediate damping and the minimum available damping settings were tried. The damping in itself was desirable but the resulting rates of roll and pitch were undesirably low for a maneuvering aircraft...

Flights were made in winds of 10 to 30 knots, including heavy gusts. The aircraft was very insensitive to gusts or wind velocity in this range, actually, and take-offs and hovering were performed at all headings to the wind. Disturbances were very minor and steady positions and headings could be held easily. Aileron 'snatching' was one highly undesirable characteristic encountered.

Fault warnings with the auto-stabilization system occurred several times. At one time a persistent roll channel fault was found to be caused by a faulty gyro. However, several spurious faults in the roll channel occurred when yawing maneuvers were attempted. These faults could be corrected by pushing a reset button while in the air...

It was not considered reasonable to land on the pit or platform since they were quite small and visibility downward was lacking at the angle required. All landings were performed over concrete. In the lower 10 feet before touchdown ground interference in addition to "suck down" was encountered. There were mild buffeting and mild, erratic upset disturbances acting on the aircraft, particularly in roll. With the auto-stabilizer system on these effects produced no perceptible requirements of the pilot for control. With the auto-stabilizer system off, the aircraft did move in response to the disturbance and the pilot had to work with moderate effort to keep the aircraft lateral translational velocities zero for the landing. It is felt that increased lateral control sensitivity (control power per inch of displacement) would reduce this effect to an imperceptible one.

Upon landing on a solid surface it was the practice to immediately shut down the lift engines because of probable damage to the concrete, and heat damage to the tires, brakes and aircraft structure. It is then the practice to windmill the engines with starting air to cool them down.

Translations over the runway to 90 knots were performed using only the propulsion engines and, then, the tilt of the lift engines. There didn't seem to be any significant difference in aircraft characteristics dependent upon the method of propulsion or lift engine tilt in the range of flight investigated. The braking provided by lift engine tilt (about ¼ "g") is effective and useful. However, the present arrangement of having a rate *actuator button on the stick and a visual position indicator at the lower left corner of the instrument panel is poor. When using the tilt in full braking for coming to a hover at a defined point it is necessary to visually locate the indicator and observe it until the tilt has been removed. A position selector type of control that gives a direct indication of the tilt position would be more desirable, it could still be retained on the stick or operated with the left hand on the throttle control. A simpler arrangement might be to have only the braking position tilt controlled through a spring loaded switch such that release of the switch would return the engine tilt to the hovering position. It would seem desirable in either of the suggested arrangements to increase the rate of engine tilt. The tilt now actuates through 35-degrees in 4 seconds, which is probably fast enough with the present arrangement...*

Visibility from the cockpit was adequate for normal hovering, and fairly steep flares to a stop from forward flight could be made without losing height or attitude reference.

It was of interest to explore the yaw control at speeds approximating those to be used by future V/STOL aircraft. Consequently, sideslips up to about 70 degrees were performed at 40 knots. At this condition, very little displacement of the yaw control was being used and the aircraft exhibited mild instability in yaw. Although the instability was apparent as a rudder force reversal it is believed that the aircraft was unstable in the control-fixed sense also. At this condition, however, full aileron was being used for lateral trim to offset a positive dihedral effect. This effect is probably dependent to a large extent on the aircraft's longitudinal attitude or angle-of-attack at the time...

At 90 knots with auto-stabilizer system on the aircraft exhibited erratic but continuous, small pitch disturbances that could be described as 'bucking'. It reminded me of an airplane with incipient wing stalling; thus, it suggested separated flow, perhaps occurring behind the lift engine intake doors. Apparently the full-autostabilized case (attitude memory included) kept the disturbances at a lower level.

At forward flight speeds, at least of the order of 30 or 40 knots, a short period, small roll oscillation was apparent. It occurred even with the auto-stabilizer system in the non-stabilized position (nozzles still controlled through the stabilizer system circuits), in which case the period seemed to be about 2 seconds. In either the rate or full-stabilized cases, the period was closer to being 1 second."[1]

As a result of more modern advancements being made in V/STOL technology, the SC-1 program was terminated in 1967. Although one of the two SC-1 aircraft had crashed in October 1963 due to a controls malfunction, killing the pilot, the SC-1 program provided aircraft developers with significant data and knowledge, particularly in the areas of stability, control, and propulsion-induced effects.

Bell X-14

Jack Reeder performing a test flight in the Bell X-14 at NASA Ames Research Center.

NASA Langley Research Center via Jack Reeder

In 1957, America attempted to develop a viable V/STOL aircraft as the Bell X-14 test-bed project sponsored by the Air Force. Control of the X-14 flight research program was transferred to NASA in 1959, and the research program and X-14 flights were led by the NASA Ames Research Center in Mountain View, California. NASA wanted as many of its V/STOL pilot experts as possible to gain experience flying the aircraft to broaden their piloting experience and contribute ideas for solutions to any handling deficiencies noted. Consequently, Langley sent Jack to perform many of the NASA test flights in the aircraft.

The X-14 used two Armstrong-Siddeley Viper jet engines, complete with a series of thrust diverters in what became known as the vectored-thrust V/STOL concept. The fuselage and tail were from a Beech T-34, and the wing was from a Beech Bonanza. The X-14 experienced many of the problems common to early V/STOL aircraft, including the phenomenon of suck-down (its landing gear had to be lengthened to minimize the problem), engine gyroscopic effects, and performance degradation due to exhaust-gas reingestion. When it was transferred to NASA, the original Viper engines were replaced with higher power GE J85s. In 1960, it was outfitted with variable-stability equipment. Thrusters at each wing tip as well as the tail were used for control at low speeds, in typical V/STOL fashion. Project researchers later noted that "during flights of the X-14 over the concrete apron at Ames the slipstream picked a heavy manhole cover out of its manhole and tossed it about like a piece of paper for a few moments underneath the aircraft. It did not contact the aircraft, fortunately. The pilot landed when he saw debris from the hole rising about him. It required two men to replace the cover."[2] The X-14 provided an enormous amount of data and information on handling qualities and aerodynamic performance. Later, it was fitted with a digital fly-by-wire control system and flew at Ames as a research vehicle until 1981.

Hawker-Siddeley P.1127

Jack Reeder's association with V/STOL aircraft reached a new high with his early involvement in what would ultimately become the most successful V/STOL airplane to date. In 1957, the British Hawker Aircraft Limited and Bristol Engine companies began development of the vectored-thrust P.1127 aircraft. The design used four thrust-vectoring nozzles and a single large turbofan engine to achieve V/STOL capability, and, rather than a test-bed objective, the project was directed at requirements for a new NATO fighter aircraft.

Unfortunately, at that time, the British government had just undergone a critical review of its advanced programs, leading to cancellation of several major activities. The government provided no funding and very limited support of the P.1127. Many skeptics in the government believed that the concept could not successfully perform a transition from hovering flight to conventional flight.

NASA test pilots Fred Drinkwater (left) and Jack Reeder (right) confer with Hawker engineer Robin Balmer about some of their flight tests in the P.1127.

NASA Langley Research Center via Jack Reeder

An international activity known as the Mutual Weapon Development Project (MWDP) of NATO had supported the project, co-funding 75 percent of the project with Bristol picking up the remaining 25 percent, but funds were rapidly being depleted. Langley's John Stack, who became an intense supporter of the concept as an active NASA member of NATO technology exchange groups, closely monitored the British activity. At Stack's initiative, wind-tunnel tests of the P.1127 design were conducted in the Langley Full Scale Tunnel. Highly successful wind-tunnel tests of a 1/6-scale free-flight model on a rapid-action outdoor crane (control-line test technique) and in the Full Scale Tunnel in early 1960 vividly demonstrated that the design could easily transition from vertical to horizontal flight, providing a substantial boost in support for the project. A critical aspect of the tests was an evaluation of the seriousness of an undesirable longitudinal "pitch up" instability caused by power induced effects on the original horizontal tail during the transition.

Jack Reeder maintaining a hover in the Hawker-Siddeley P.1127 in England in 1962.

NASA Langley Research Center via Jack Reeder

The NASA tests showed that the pitch-up phenomenon was controllable. These tests were conducted before the airplane attempted a transition flight. Langley also assisted the project with tests in the 16-Foot Transonic Tunnel, designed to determine a fix for the pitch-up tendency at transonic speeds. As a result of these and other tests, the horizontal tail surfaces of the P.1127 were modified with anhedral ("droop") to cure the problem. Sir Sydney Camm, famous designer of the P.1127 (as well as the British Hurricane, Typhoon, and Hunter aircraft) would later say that "The only model tests that were worthwhile in the project were those of the NASA at Langley!"[3]

The first untethered hover of a P.1127 was made in November 1960, and the first conventional flight was made in July 1961. Control power was low about all axes, which, combined with suck-down and limited height control power, resulted in a high pilot workload in low-speed flight. In late 1961, a full evaluation of the P.1127 by a team of U.S. Air Force and Army pilots had been proposed, but Hawker submitted a strong counter-proposal to have "NASA pilots such as Reeder or Drinkwater (Fred Drinkwater, Ames test pilot) conduct the assessment. It is essential to have someone with the right technical background rather than a military test team at this point."[4] Subsequently, Reeder was personally invited by Hawker chief test pilot Bill Bedford to fly the P.1127.[5] Interestingly, Bedford did not mention the fact that he had successfully ejected from the second P.1127 during a crash from hovering flight a few weeks before!

Jack Reeder and Ames test pilot Fred Drinkwater went to England to fly the P.1127 in 1962, collaborating with Hawker test pilots Bedford and Hugh Merewether on solutions to the flight operational problems. Reeder later recorded some of the early thoughts concerning the P.1127:

> *I was shown a complete movie history of the flights to date. Lift-off over the pit was accomplished at a thrust-to-weight ratio of about 1.1. A strong 'suck-down' force has been experienced over solid runway, reducing this ratio to about 1.0. The early impression of the pilots was that height control was their major problem. Consequently, a throttle mechanism has been installed that allows about an inch of throttle travel at twice the normal gearing for vernier control after the course adjustment has been made. This seems to have helped the height control.*
>
> *Another early problem encountered was due to the outrigger wheels allowing the aircraft*

to lean one way or the other. As thrust was increased, the side force created by the landing gear at the ground produced upsetting moments that the roll control could not overcome. This was partially corrected by adding extensions to the outriggers, and further extensions are thought desirable for future hovering. Even after the main gear is off the ground, though, the nose wheel may still be in contact and has caused uncontrollable yawing and rolling when lateral drift occurred. Consequently, an indication for adjusting to the right longitudinal attitude of lift-off and hovering is needed."[6]

XV-6 Kestrel

NASA Langley test pilot Lee Person maintaining a hover in the XV-6 Kestrel at NASA Langley in 1966.

NASA Langley Research Center

In 1962, the United Kingdom, United States, and Germany initiated a tripartite program, funding nine improved P.1127 aircraft known as Kestrels for use in international operational trials. The Kestrel was designated the XV-6 in the U.S. inventory, and aircraft were to be evaluated by the Air Force, Army, and Navy. In 1966, the tripartite evaluations ended and NASA acquired two XV-6 aircraft for flight research studies. Langley test pilot Lee Person was assigned as lead test pilot for the studies, with Reeder serving as his technical mentor.

These studies were among the first to explore the use of thrust vectoring in forward flight for enhanced air combat maneuverability, proving the viability of the Vectoring in Forward Flight (VIFF) concept.

The P.1127 and Kestrel designs ultimately evolved into the highly successful Harrier design used by the British Royal Navy and Air Force, and the United States Marines Corps AV-8B.

Yet another approach to providing V/STOL capability flown by Reeder involved the tilt-wing concept. During the 1950s, researchers at Langley investigated the feasibility of the pivoting and tilting the wing of a propeller-driven aircraft from a conventional horizontal attitude (for cruise flight) to a vertical position relative to the fuselage (for hovering flight). The key technical approach was to prevent wing stall by immersing most of the wing in the high-energy slipstream of rather large propellers. Extensive model tests were conducted in wind-tunnels, and free-flight models were also used to explore the concept.

The researchers confirmed in their studies that the transition between conventional and hovering flight sometimes produced an undesirable and potentially dangerous wing stall accompanied by random wing dropping, particularly for low-power, descending conditions. Solutions to the problem required a careful selection of wing airfoil sections and high-lift devices.

Vertol VZ-2

Under the auspices of the Army and the Office of Naval Research, a small, inexpensive research aircraft, known as the VZ-2, was built by Vertol to explore the tilt-wing concept in flight. The aircraft was initially flown in 1957, made the world's first conversion by a tilt-wing aircraft on July 15, 1958, and was assigned to the NASA Langley Research Center in 1959 for flight studies. Jack Reeder was tasked with the job of serving as lead test pilot on the project.

Jack Reeder prepares to make a short takeoff in the Vertol VZ-2 at NASA Langley in 1962.

NASA Langley Research Center

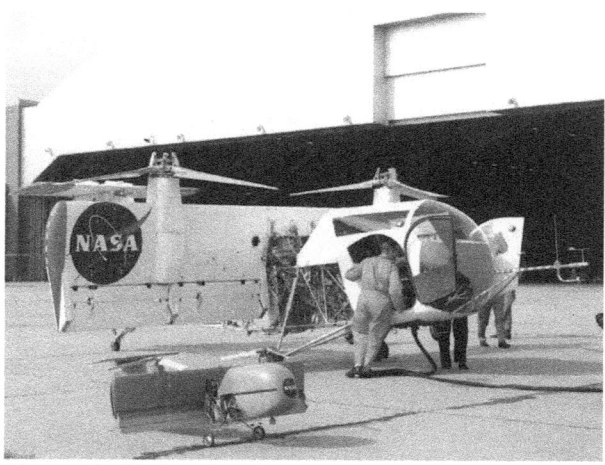

1962 display at NASA Langley showing the VZ-2 test aircraft and VZ-2 free flight model studied in the Full Scale Wind Tunnel.

NASA Langley Research Center

During the test flights, Jack quickly experienced the anticipated problems associated with wing stall when flying the unflapped-wing version of the aircraft during descending flight. The problem was manifested by heavy buffeting and roll-off motions, and was later corrected by incorporating a drooped wing leading-edge and a full-span trailing-edge wing flap. Reeder also noted that the airplane did not operate as smoothly when performing a hover close to the ground, particularly in gusty conditions. To correct the problem, an artificial rate stabilization system was incorporated, which greatly reduced pilot workload.

The VZ-2 flight program was one of the most successful V/STOL projects in the U.S., completing over 35 transitions from hover to cruise and back. Jack and other pilots contributed to the general design data base for future V/STOL airplanes, generating an enormous amount of information on the aerodynamics of wing/propeller interactions, and handling quality evaluations.

LTV-Hiller-Ryan XC-142A and Canadair CL-84

LTV-Hiller-Ryan XC-142A performing a vertical takeoff at NASA Langley in 1968.

NASA Langley Research Center

Canadair CL-84 in vertical flight mode.

NASA Langley Research Center via Jack Reeder

Jack in the CL-84 prior to performing a test flight.

Jack Reeder via NASA Langley Research Center

One program that benefited from the earlier NASA research was the four-engine, propeller-driven LTV-Hiller-Ryan XC-142A tilt-wing transport, developed for the U.S. military. After military evaluations, an XC-142A was turned over to Langley for research test flights from October 1968 to May 1970. The lead pilot for the XC-142A program at Langley was pilot Bob Champine, who was head of the pilots' section.

Jack performing a test flight in the CL-84.
Jack Reeder via NASA Langley Research Center

Also, in the 1960s, the tilt-wing V/STOL concept was adopted in the design of the twin-engine, propeller-driven Canadian Canadair CL-84. The aircraft was initially flown in 1965, and thoroughly tested in Canada throughout the late 1960s. Jack Reeder and Bob Champine travelled to Canada to participate in flight studies of the aircraft and assist the Canadians in the development of their tilt-wing test bed. The following trip report provides an account of their evaluation of the CL-84:

"Mssrs. R. A. Champine and J. P. Reeder of the NASA Langley Research Center visited Canadair, Limited, during the period from October 11 through October 17, 1966, for the purpose of making a brief engineering evaluation of the aircraft in the

light of NASA's past V/STOL experience.

The CL-84 aircraft has a design gross weight for STOL operations of 14,700 pounds. For the NASA flights, the weight, suitable for VTOL flight, was 11,200 pounds at take off with 1000 pounds of fuel and about 1000 pounds of instrumentation. Mr. Longhurst of Canadair served as safety pilot in the right seat on all flights. Temperatures varied from 67° F to as low as 38° F. At 63° F the thrust/weight ratio at take-off was estimated to be 1.10. Seven evaluation flights were made by the two NASA pilots, three by Champine and four by Reeder.

The winds encountered for the NASA flights were generally high. The lightest winds encountered were about 10 mph with gusts to 15 or 20 mph on two flights. Otherwise, winds were from 15 mph to 25 mph, with gusts to 40 mph. Under test conditions, all hovering flight was done in winds of 10 mph or greater. During all vertical take offs and landings and below a wheel height of about 15 feet there was considerable buffeting of the aircraft structure, and suck down (negative ground effect) was evident on landing. Buffeting was evident as high as 30 feet, on occasions, when full power was added to correct for settling. Although wing drop had been reported at 25 knots in outbound conversion below 15 feet, none was encountered in our flights at any height with winds from 10 mph to 40 mph. The aircraft actually exhibited no upset disturbances of appreciable magnitude about any axis during the operations, despite the airframe buffeting. However, on vertical landings the aircraft occasionally tended to slide sideways to the right when a few feet from the ground.

This was corrected readily with a lateral attitude change before making ground contact. Wing tilt had to be used, keeping the fuselage essentially level, to prevent backward or forward drift of the aircraft as either the takeoff or landing progressed. The wind gradients in the lower 15 to 20 feet of altitude were always apparent. Above about 15-foot wheel height the aircraft became very steady with very low vibration level. The major effect of wind gusts when heading into the wind was slow drift of the aircraft backward or forward that a short blip of the wing-tilt switch could correct. No appreciable accelerations along the longitudinal axis due to the gusts were felt. The hovering roll rate available with lateral SAS on was felt to be more sluggish than desirable for maneuvering (Cooper 4) and full lateral throw of the stick was reached in maneuvers that were only a little more severe than normal ones. Control for the steady hovering only was very good (Cooper 2).

With lateral SAS off, the control power and roll velocity capability for maneuvering were good with satisfactorily little overshoot (Cooper 2), except that there seems to be a detectable lag (transport plus first order, perhaps) in the initiation of response. This caused no problem, however. There was an uncomfortable feeling that a dangerous PIO (pilot induced oscillation) could result from coupling with sideslip velocity with SAS off, however (Cooper 5). A controls-fixed lateral oscillation was tried and indicated that the oscillation, estimated to be of about 5-seconds period, doubled amplitude rapidly, perhaps in one-half cycle. Because of apprehension, this trial oscillation was damped at the end of a one-half cycle, requiring full control. This tended to substantiate the feeling that a highly dangerous PIO could easily result if maneuvers involving sideslip velocities were executed without caution with the SAS off. A gain of 0.4 of maximum for the roll damping gave more desirable roll control response and rolling velocity than maximum gain, but did permit some lateral wobbling in hovering. It was then noted that the lateral rate gain had to be turned up to full to eliminate all lateral wobbling during hover...

Wing tilt is a primary control at low speed, but its use is logical and easy except that the upward rate of 6° per second (to reduce speed) is about half the downward rate near hover. The downward rate was desirable (Cooper 2), but the upward rate was too slow (Cooper 4). Forward on the wing switch for downward wing tilt was easy to use, whereas rearward actuation was difficult for the thumb without loosening the grip on the power lever or moving the lever aft inadvertently. The wing actually stuck a time or two when trying to actuate it upward, and a jar was felt as it broke free. The low rate, the awkwardness of switch actuation and occasional sticking led to doubt as to whether the wing was actually operating in the up direction at times. Following maneuvers during which wing tilt was used, non-level fuselage attitude frequently resulted. Confusion as to which way to move the wing to level the fuselage then resulted until, (1) the wing position indicator was consulted; (2) a rule of thumb such as moving the switch in the same direction as the aircraft nose was displaced was applied; or (3) the expedient of leveling the aircraft and using wing tilt to counter the translation was applied. Method (3) was the one preferred, generally...

In conventional flight mode, as an airplane up to 200 knots cruise the aircraft was quite good overall (Cooper 2-1/2). The force per 'g' was low, but with 17 percent static margin the aircraft felt solid and positive with adequate stick displacements required for longitudinal maneuvers. The response to step displace-and-hold elevator inputs was good (Cooper 2) with no overshoot.

The rolling velocity capability with SAS on and set at normal gain was sluggish (Cooper 4). Roll response and the rolling velocity capability with the roll SAS off was very good (Cooper 1) and there was no overshoot...

> *On two of the later flights in the aircraft an increasing yawing moment with speed was encountered that was trimmed out with the directional trim system that readjusts the pitch of the two propellers differentially. This yawing moment was apparently caused by a trim adjustment made to the propellers for hovering flight. On the second flight of the two referred to, the yawing moment due to the propellers was cut in half by a readjustment, thus indicating that careful adjustment can alleviate the problem.*
>
> *Although high winds prevailed during our flights the turbulence encountered at test altitudes, approximately 2,000 to 4,000 feet, was light. In this air, the aircraft rode smoothly with very minor disturbances except for one pronounced jolt which was encountered in cruise with about 85 percent rpm and thought to be a combined deceleration and yaw to the right. It was assumed to be the effects of a horizontal gust on axial propeller forces, and is of interest only because there has been discussions in the past about gust effects on propellers with large blade areas. It was concluded from our experience in the CL-84 that this effect is of no concern…*
>
> *In conclusion, the aircraft seems excellently engineered and has outstandingly good handling qualities for its type, even with SAS off. One area of concern does exist, however; the corridor defined by stall effects in descent at a typical STOL operating speed, 40 knots, does not seem wide enough for service use by operational pilots. For instance, it did not seem possible to set up a reasonable rate of descent of 500 fpm without encountering 'divergent settling' which necessitated enough added power for recovery after a few seconds to destroy descent path control. It is felt that at least 1,000 fpm steady descent capability should be available for corrections to flight path for an operational aircraft.*
>
> *Other than the concern over the descent limitation it is felt that this aircraft is suitable for an evaluation in the field with operational pilots."*[9]

Following the NASA test pilot evaluations, the CL-84 program suffered a setback when the test aircraft was lost in an accident caused by engine problems during transition. The military services sought to exploit the capabilities of the aircraft and purchased three, with one being evaluated by the U.S. Navy in 1970. The Navy evaluation process included the successful performance of aircraft carrier trials. The CL-84 continued to positively influence military officials; however, the military made no plans to adopt the aircraft type for routine use.

Curtiss-Wright X-100

Jack Reeder flying the Curtiss-Wright X-100 tilt-propeller test bed. (Jack Reeder via NASA Langley Research Center)

NASA Langley Research Center via Jack Reeder

During the latter 1950s, radical new V/STOL designs used yet another form of propulsion known as the tilt-propeller concept. In this approach, rudimentary wings remained fixed and the propellers turned or tilted to change the flight mode. The concept materialized in the form of the Curtiss-Wright X-100, which made its first flight in 1960. One objective of the X-100 program was to demonstrate and evaluate Curtiss-Wright's concept of using propeller "radial force" instead of wing lift for conventional flight. Properly designed propellers can produce large forces when inclined at angle of attack, and the magnitude of the force can provide substantial lift. The X-100 used engine exhaust for pitch and yaw control in hovering flight, and roll control was provided by differential propeller pitch. The X-100 made its first (and only) transition from vertical to horizontal flight in April 1960.

At the end of 1960, Curtiss-Wright transferred the X-100 to NASA Langley, where it underwent testing for a year. Jack found that the control effectiveness of the X-100 at low speeds was very weak, and the problem was never resolved; however, the focus of the test program was on the effects of high velocity prop-wash on varied types of landing surfaces, such as packed dirt, grass, snow, and pavement. The X-100 only flew in the vertical flight mode during the NASA evaluation, and spent most of its time tethered to the ground.

First Tilt-Rotor Aircraft XV-3

XV-3 tilt rotor research aircraft in hovering flight at NASA Ames Research Center.

NASA Ames Research Center

Jack's flight time in V/STOL aircraft also included one of the first tilt-rotor aircraft known as the XV-3. The tilt-rotor concept involves the use of large-diameter rotors on engine nacelles that transition from vertical to conventional mode in flight. In 1955, the Bell Helicopter Company developed a tiltrotor test bed for use by the Army and Air Force. It made its first flight as a helicopter in August 1955, but crashed two months later before completing a full conversion. After the crash, extensive wind-tunnel and ground-based tests were conducted, and piloting tasks during the conversion to forward flight were reviewed and rehearsed. Bell consulted with NASA on how to correct the problems and a flight research program was initiated at Ames Research Center. In 1958, Jack Reeder evaluated the XV-3 at Ames. Jack later compared the XV-3 to another V/STOL aircraft that he gained considerable experience in at the time, the Vertol VZ-2 tilt-wing test bed:

> *"The XV-3 aircraft seems to suffer very much less than the VZ-2 from downwash-ground interference. However, there are erratic disturbances in roll that produce the impression of wing stalling. Slow adverse yawing sometimes occurs simultaneously, also. Roll control, provided by differential collective pitch as for the VZ-2, is adequate in power. No force gradients in roll are provided, but some friction has been intentionally added. There is some tendency to over-control, but the control is not as touchy as the VZ-2. I think the erratic wing dropping is more responsible for the tendency to over-control than the control characteristics themselves. I think that force gradients or 'feel' would improve control.*
>
> *Control power and damping in pitch for the XV-3 are low enough to be considered only marginally satisfactory. As for roll, only a friction force is provided in the longitudinal control system. No difficulties are encountered about the pitch axis in still air hovering, however. Control power in yaw is entirely inadequate and damping poor. Control moments in this case are derived from differential cyclic feathering and are compromised in the design with the feathering demands for longitudinal control. This axis is of least importance in hovering and causes little concern. However, the lack of yaw control might become a problem in gusty winds. It is important to note that the XV-3 does not have stability augmentation about any axis."*[8]

The XV-3 flight-test program proved the practicality of the tilt-rotor, however, difficulties including rotor performance, aerodynamic instability of the aircraft design, and undesirable blade characteristics during flight were encountered. The Army and NASA at Ames later corrected these problems in the more advanced Bell XV-15 tilt-rotor test bed that they successfully flew. This research program directly contributed to the development of the V-22 Osprey in service today with the U.S. Marine Corps.

Doak VZ-4

Doak VZ-4 ducted fan test bed at NASA Langley in 1960.
NASA Langley Research Center

Another type of V/STOL aircraft flown by Reeder used the tilt-duct concept, in which multi-bladed propellers are mounted in tiltable ducts at the wing tips. The Doak Aircraft Company of Torrance, California advocated this concept. In 1958, the Army and later NASA began flight research studies of the Doak VZ-4, which used eight-bladed 4-ft diameter propellers within tilting ducts at its wingtips. A single engine drove the ducted props. Controllable inlet guide vanes provided roll control during hovering flight, and engine exhaust gases were deflected at the rear of the fuselage for pitch and yaw control. The Army accepted the VZ-4 in September 1959, and transferred it to Langley for further tests. Langley conducted wind-tunnel tests to support the activity, and Jack flew the flight-test program. Jack had the following thoughts about flying this aircraft:

> "The Doak aircraft is now supposed to have adequate control for hover, but time history data and visual observation would tend to indicate less than desirable control power in roll, particularly. During hovering, and particularly in a slight vertical descent, continuous left and right controlling with as much as ½ available throw is shown in some time histories. Pitch control frequently shows use of ½ deflection inputs also. The Doak aircraft, as in the case of the XV-3, has no stability augmentation system...
>
> The transition from hovering flight to airplane flight is readily accomplished with the VZ-2, XV-3, Doak and X-14 with some limitations. Greater limitations generally exist for the return from airplane flight to hovering, however. The Doak has proven to have a serious limitation in this regard."[9]

Test pilots, including Reeder, found that the aircraft exhibited stalling of the duct inlet lips, and the ducted propellers when performing the transition from vertical to conventional flight produced a large nose-up trim change. Supplemental research conducted in Langley wind tunnels yielded an option that corrected the problem. The correction involved adding control vanes within the ducts. The flight program proved to be hazardous when one of the ducted fan engines caught fire. Upon landing, Reeder had to be pulled from the aircraft by ground crews. Nevertheless, the VZ-4 flight-test program demonstrated the potential advantages of the tilt-duct concept, causing the Navy to invest in the more advanced Bell X-22A, which served as a highly successful tilt-duct test bed even though the Navy never adopted the type for standard use.

The excitement and promise of V/STOL aircraft – with the exception of continued maturity of the P.1127 into the Harrier and AV-8 concepts – began to cool on an international scale by the 1970s. The complexity of such aircraft, coupled with the penalties associated with V/STOL performance, and noise proved to be unacceptable to potential users of the technology, resulting in massive cancellations and termination of existing V/STOL programs.

Time-lapse photography showing the various stages of transition from vertical to conventional flight mode for the Doak VZ-4.

Doak via Jack Reeder via NASA Langley Research Center

Chapter Seven Notes

1. Reeder, John P. (July 1962). "Flights in Short SC-1 Aircraft at Bedford, England" as found in V/STOL Aircraft with which NASA Langley has had Piloting Experience. National Aeronautics and Space Administration, Langley Research Center, Hampton, Va., pp. 1–2 and 4–6.

2. V/STOL Aircraft with which NASA Langley has had Piloting Experience. National Aeronautics and Space Administration, Langley Research Center, Hampton, Va., p. 19.

3. Letter from Robert B. Marsh, Hawker Aircraft Limited, to Marion O. McKinney, September 15, 1961.

4. Letter from Robert B. Marsh, Hawker Aircraft Limited, to Marion O. McKinney, December 13, 1961.

5. Letter from Bill Bedford, Hawker Aircraft Limited, to John P. Reeder, December 27, 1961.

6. V/STOL Aircraft with which NASA Langley has had Piloting Experience. National Aeronautics and Space Administration, Langley Research Center, Hampton, Va., p. 7.

7. Reeder, John P. and Champine, Robert A. (November 30, 1966). "Langley Working Paper (LWP)-331: Flight Evaluation of Canadair CL-84 Tilt-Wing V/STOL Aircraft by NASA Pilots" as found in V/STOL Aircraft with which NASA Langley has had Piloting Experience. National Aeronautics and Space Administration, Langley Research Center, Hampton, Va., pp. 1–7 and 13.

8. Reeder, John P. and Drinkwater, Fred J. III (February 2, 1960). "Limited Flight Experience with Several Types of VTOL Aircraft" as found in <u>V/STOL Aircraft with which NASA Langley has had Piloting Experience</u>. National Aeronautics and Space Administration, Langley Research Center, Hampton, Va., p. 3.

9. Ibid., pp. 4 and 5.

Chapter Eight
The Future of
Air Transportation:
THE TERMINAL CONFIGURED VEHICLE
PROGRAM

Jack Reeder speaking at a Flight Safety Foundation, Inc. meeting about Langley's TCV program and the issue of flight safety.
NASA Langley Research Center via Jack Reeder

Center Director Edgar Cortright congratulates Jack Reeder after delivering a speech about Langley's TCV Program efforts.

NASA Langley Research Center via Jack Reeder

From 1963 until 1970, Jack Reeder served Langley as the Assistant Chief of the Flight Mechanics and Technology Division. His assignment to the position was due directly to the strong opinion of Philip Donely, Chief of the Division, that Reeder's expertise and leadership qualities needed to be moved to a higher level of management and leadership potential. While serving in the position, Jack continued his overview and interests in V/STOL and rotorcraft research, but his primary interest was beginning to change to a new technical area, brought about by the rapid growth in the U.S. civil transport industry and the shortcomings of the existing air traffic control system that were becoming evident. With his broad experiences in pilot/airplane/air traffic interactions, he could readily anticipate the coming problems, including airport congestion and flight delays (particularly in inclement weather). Jack knew that providing solutions to the emerging problems would require not only NASA's advanced technologies for aircraft, but also unprecedented levels of close cooperation and partnering with the Federal Aviation Administration (FAA) air traffic control system, industry, and international regulatory agencies. He began to advocate for such a vision, speaking of delivering a "chock-to-chock" capability in all-weather conditions.

In 1970, Director Edgar M. Cortright reorganized NASA Langley, and Jack became the Chief of the Research Aircraft Flight Division, a position he held for about three and a half years. During this period, he reported to his friend, Larry Loftin, who served as the Director of Aeronautics. Meanwhile, Jack's previous duties as Head of Flight Operations were taken over by James M. Patton, Jr.

Reeder's growing interest in an obvious need for advanced civil cockpit technology and operational capabilities in and near the airport, or terminal area, came at an opportune time for the agency. NASA and the Department of Transportation had been charged by Congress to examine the current and future state of the civil air transportation system, and to recommend research efforts to ensure that the system remained healthy

NASA Langley's Boeing B-737 TCV research aircraft as it appeared at Langley in 1973.

NASA Langley Research Center via Larry Loftin

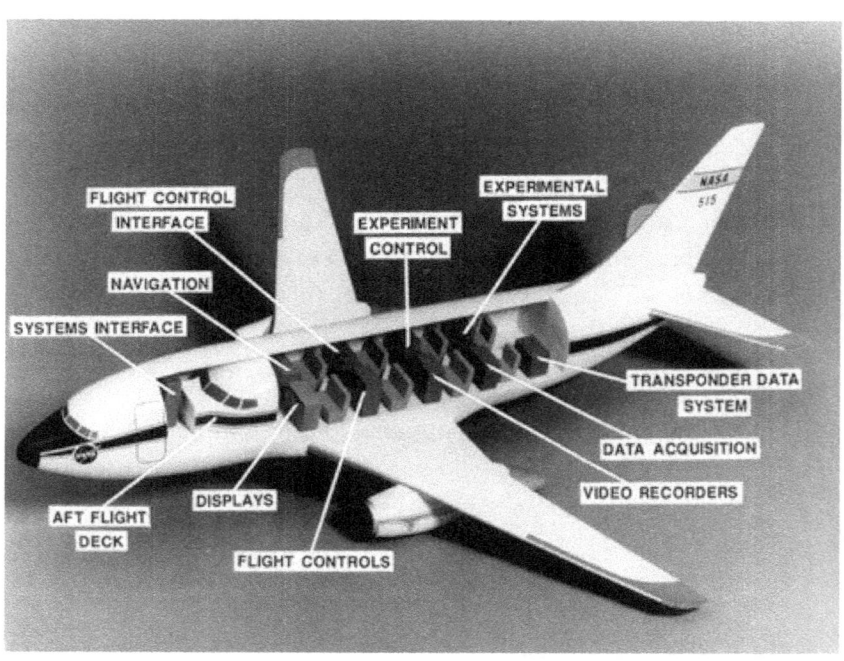

NASA Boeing B-737 TCV research aircraft cutaway model showing aft flight deck and aircraft systems.

NASA Langley Research Center

and robust. Jack and Langley's G. Barry Graves, Jr. (then Head of the Flight Instrumentation Division) spearheaded a common vision for a new research program that would integrate critical aspects of the interactions between the pilot/airplane interface, as well as the operational interactions of the pilot/airplane combination with the air traffic control system. The new program would ultimately be known as the Terminal Configured Vehicle (TCV) Program. The program included analysis, piloted simulation, and flight-testing to research and develop advanced flight-control and cockpit-display concepts, and other enabling technologies that would permit new options in flight operations and would expedite all-weather operations. The envisioned scope of studies would include time-controlled navigation with transition to the new microwave landing system (MLS) and permit precision curved, steep, decelerating, time-sequenced final approaches as well as low-visibility landings through turnoff.

Boeing B-737 TCV

To accomplish these goals in a realistic, integrated fashion required an extensive replication of real-world operational features that could only be provided by a research airplane. Following successful advocacy efforts by jack and others, NASA acquired a Boeing 737 transport (the original prototype 737) for the TCV Program on July 26, 1973. After its acquisition, the airplane was modified and equipped with advanced avionics systems, including a digital implementation of the navigation and guidance functions, cathode ray tube displays of the vertical and horizontal situation, and a triplex digital control system. The aircraft was also equipped with an innovative fly-by-wire research cockpit located in the main cabin area behind the normal aircraft cockpit. The research cockpit was used to evaluate advanced concepts, with primary flight safety delegated to a safety pilot flying in the front cockpit.

Immediately prior to the arrival of the 737, Langley faced the issue of which research organization would manage the facility. On the one hand, a new Director for Aeronautics, Robert E. Bower, was managing the traditional aeronautics work and avionics research was led by Barry

Graves, who had risen to the position of Director of Electronics. After considerable deliberations, the TCV project was assigned to the Electronics Directorate under Graves in May 1973. Jack Reeder was assigned to the position of Chief of the Terminal Configured Vehicle (TCV) Program Office, and launched into his new duties with energy and excitement. The necessary relationships with the FAA and industry were promoted and successfully acquired, and an extremely important commitment was made by Boeing to commit a team of engineers and technicians to the Langley site for common assistance and technology transfer.

Noted author Lane E. Wallace presents an excellent, detailed account of Langley's experiences and contributions with its 737 flight research aircraft and its two decades of contributions in <u>Airborne Trailblazer: Two Decades with NASA Langley's 737 Flying Laboratory</u> (NASA SP-4216), and the reader is referred to that outstanding publication for more details of the numerous accomplishments of the program.

Extremely relevant advanced technologies were developed during the TCV Program, including a Time Reference Scanning Beam (TRSB) MLS, which ultimately enhanced the all-weather landing capability of large commercial jetliners. Reeder and Langley test pilots Lee Person and Dick Yenni flew the airplane, equipped with the new technology, in demonstration flights in heavily congested airspaces above Montreal, Canada; New York City; Denver, Colorado; and Buenos Aires, Argentina. The success of the flight tests led to the adoption of the technology by the International Civil Aviation Organization (ICAO) as a replacement for the obsolescent instrument landing system (ILS) still widely in use at the time.[1]

Another outstanding contribution of the program resulted from the stimulation and advocacy for "glass cockpit" displays now commonly used in civil and military aircraft. With Boeing engineers on site and interfacing with real-time results from Langley research on advanced display concepts, the word was spread back to senior Boeing management regarding the impressive capabilities provided by the innovative glass cockpit concepts. This internal pressure to adopt the new technology was ultimately adopted by Boeing management for all new products since the 757 and 767.

Jack Reeder's success in helping to bring the 737 to Langley was, arguably, his most important contribution to the Langley Research Center. Not only did the airplane become a vital facility used for aeronautics research for over 20 years, it served to stimulate a new influx of cockpit-display research that literally paved the way for Langley to be recognized as the U.S. leader in the field.

One unexpected benefit of Jack's efforts to implement the TCV technology studies involved Langley's personnel that were involved in rotorcraft research during the early 1970s. At that time, Langley had continued its world-class studies in rotorcraft aerodynamics, structures, and flying qualities with a full plate of exciting projects, including the unique Rotor Systems Research Aircraft (RSRA) Program and the VTOL Approach and Landing Technology (VALT) Program. The joint NASA/Army RSRA program began in the early 1970s to provide a "flying wind tunnel" to investigate ways to increase the speed of rotorcraft, as well as their performance, reliability, and safety. It also sought to reduce the noise, vibration, and maintenance costs of helicopters. Sikorsky Aircraft Division of United Technologies Laboratories built two RSRA aircraft under contract to Langley. The VALT Program was a concerted effort by Langley researchers using a CH-47 research helicopter to establish technology for rotorcraft operation in a terminal area environment, including automatic, decelerating approach to landings.

Unfortunately, another headquarters decision brought these programs to a sudden conclusion at Langley when, in 1976, the decision was made to move all rotorcraft flight research to the Ames Research Center. As would be expected, the impact on personal lives, morale, and futures of the affected researchers was enormous. Many researchers were determined not to transfer to Ames, and the agency was facing the loss of experienced, highly trained personnel. Fortunately, Jack had brought the necessary ingredients together to transition the otherwise excess researchers to a new program, known as the Cockpit Display of Traffic Integration (CDTI) Program. The backgrounds of most of the researchers had involved world-class expertise in cockpit displays and control strategies; and their talents were a perfect fit to the new program.

Above: NASA Boeing B-737 TCV research aircraft front flight deck prior to incorporation of TCV program glass cockpit displays, flight instruments and controls, and advanced avionics equipment. Below: TCV flight deck after incorporation of TCV program glass cockpit displays.

NASA Langley Research Center

Jack Reeder continued to manage the TCV Program as it contributed not only technology, but also a culture of NASA/FAA/Industry cooperation that was monumental in designing the course of similar projects in coming decades. Jack retired from NASA in December 1980, having completed a highly productive 42-year career. After his retirement, Thomas Walsh initially managed the TCV Program, and its name was changed to the Advanced Transport Operating Systems (ATOPS). The seeds planted by Jack's efforts continued to grow, and a long list of contributions poured from the program over the 1980s and 1990s. Advanced communication concepts, system monitoring concepts, displays, and wind-shear avoidance technology were all successfully researched and improved. The 737 was finally retired by NASA in 1997, after completing one of the most noteworthy careers of a research airplane.

Dick Yenni, Jack Reeder, Tom Walsh, and Lee Person confer beside Langley's TCV B-737.

NASA Langley Research Center via Jack Reeder

Jack Reeder being interviewed by a local Tidewater, Virginia, area news Station crew about Langley's TCV Program.

NASA Langley Research Center via Larry Loftin

Jack Reeder watches as Fred Drinkwater prepares to perform a test flight in the P.1127.

NASA Langley Research Center via Jack Reeder

Jack Reeder (right) receiving the NASA Outstanding Leadership Medal from Dr. Alan Lovelace, Deputy NASA Administrator, in 1978 after NASA Langley successfully demonstrated the U.S. Microwave Landing System (MLS) to I.C.A.O. worldwide.

NASA Langley Research Center via Jack Reeder

Chapter Eight Notes

1. John White, <u>SAE Technical Paper Series #901969: Advanced Transport Operating Systems Program</u>. Warrendale, PA: Society of Automotive Engineers, Inc., 1990.

Jack receives his NASA 40-year service award in 1978 from Director Donald P. Hearth.

NASA Langley Research Center via Jack Reeder

Chapter Nine
Jack Reeder's Legacy

Herb Fisher Don R. Berlin Scott Crossfield Tony LeVier L. Child John Seal M/Gen. Foulois Pete Jansen Roscoe Turner Vance Breese Dean Smith Jack Reeder

Jack's professional association included the most notable test pilots in the world. Here, he is attending a meeting of the Society of Experimental Test Pilots with notable friends.

Jack Reeder

Any attempt to summarize the extraordinary career of Jack Reeder presents a formidable challenge. His leadership and personal interest in aviation, combined with his engineering and test pilot background, enabled him to contribute vital information to a broad variety of aircraft, including conventional fixed-wing aircraft, rotorcraft, and V/STOL aircraft. He contributed data, evaluations, and guidelines that have continued to contribute today in the fields of aerodynamics, stability and control, guidance and display systems, and operational procedures. He was truly a legend in the NACA/NASA culture.

In the course of gathering material for this book, interviews with Jack's peers, associates, and subordinates solidified a common perspective on his personal dedication to his research activities and to those he worked with. Throughout his career at Langley, Reeder passed on invaluable insights, work habits, and a sense of camaraderie and work ethics that benefited future generations of engineers and test pilots. Reeder's analytical mindset when flying test aircraft and his unique application of engineering insight was especially noticed by the other pilots, and influenced their own approach to being a test pilot.

Testimony to the impact of Jack Reeder on individual personal careers from his peers would literally take volumes of space and is far beyond the scope of this publication. However, several comments are provided to reemphasize the esteem that his fellow researchers bestowed on him.

Former Langley flight research pilot Lee Person said:

> *"He was my hero. He could fly anything, and tell you how it could be improved so anybody could fly it. Jack was so smart, you could go out and fly with him and he could show you things about airplanes you never even would think about. I had been*

instructed for about 200 hours in the T-28 Trojan trainer at Pensacola in the Navy Flight Training Program and he told me things about the T-28 I never would have even imagined, especially with regard to the aileron control forces with flaps up and flaps down. I never had even thought about it, and he was right. When I looked at it he was exactly right. I remember another magnificent contribution, when Jack and Fred Drinkwater from Ames fine-tuned the flying qualities of the Kestrel V/STOL airplane and the resulting hovering characteristics of that airplane were absolutely superb with regard to control forces and moments, stick displacements and control harmony. I never got to fly the P-51B, but evidently he had done the same thing with that airplane during the 1940s. It was always fun to go flying with Jack, because he could make aircraft perform like no one else. A good example occurred one day when we were flying the H-13 helicopter. He was checking me out so I could fly helicopters, and all of the sudden he barely got the helicopter off the ground, pulled back on the stick, and the nose came up about 60° as he rotated it off across the top so that the helicopter was pointing 60° toward the ground and I swallowed my heart. I never tried that maneuver, but I was really impressed that he could do it.

Lee Person and Jack Reeder pose in front of two Kestrel V/STOL airplanes used in NASA research programs in 1966.

NASA Langley Research Center

Jack was a wonderful boss. He would give you a job and let you do it and not tell you exactly what to do. When the Tripartite Test Program shut down and Langley inherited a couple of the Kestrels for flight research, Jack assigned me as a pilot on that program and said 'Lee I want you to go out and sit there in the airplane and add a little thrust, get it a little light on the struts, and feel out the controls.' So I got it a little light on the struts, and lifted it up a little and took a little turn out into the wind. Then I took the thrust off, and it fell back onto the ground. So I tried it again and the same thing happened. So I took the thrust off and instead of getting it light, I added a whole bunch of thrust and the airplane popped right off the ground. I hovered it there for a couple of minutes, and put it back down on the ground and shut it down. I got out of the airplane and made my way to the door of the Flight Research Office and Jack met me there. Invariably, he prefixed some of his messages with some curse words and he said 'Lee I told you just to get it light on the struts, I didn't tell you to fly it!' I said 'Well Jack, I tried that a couple of times and it didn't work very well, so I thought if I could get it up off the ground a couple of times, I might be able to fly it well.' Jack said 'Well that's what I would have done, but I didn't expect you to do that, I expected you to do exactly what I told you to do!' Jack was the Head of the Pilot's Office when I got to NASA and he always kept us working fine together all the time. He mainly wanted us to do airplane-related things, but he had to loan us to the Space Program as well, so we did that."[1]

Reeder always attempted to get as much technical information as possible from every valuable minute of flight test. This was evident in his general approach to a flight- test evaluation, including his habit of taking extensive notes on the flying qualities of aircraft after performing test flights. Bob Tapscott, a key leader of Langley's rotorcraft programs, commented: "After completing a test flight in a rotorcraft, Jack would pause 10–15 minutes to make copious notes to himself and for other pilots and engineers to use for reference."[2]

Another noted researcher in the rotorcraft program, John Garren, observed:

"As a test subject in our handling qualities research efforts using variable stability aircraft, he was without peer, providing comprehensive commentary, both verbal and written. It was not unusual, even days after the flight debriefing, for him to come by the office with additional comments and thoughts. There was never any doubt about

> his genuine interest in, and dedication to our research efforts. Even more valuable, however – I believe actually crucial to our programmatic success – was his guidance and advocacy. Moreover, he was always the gentleman, respected for his character and technical competence everywhere.
>
> One example of his invaluable contributions to our research involved the issue of using 'bang-bang' (full-on or full-off) control for NASA's Lunar Lander Vehicle. Jack had attended a meeting early in the Apollo Program where a discussion had ensued concerning whether a pilot could execute an approach to a hover and landing using an on/off control system for pitch and roll. There were many in the pilot community who thought it would not be possible. Being quite familiar with our recent development of the 'model-following' simulation technique on our CH-46 variable stability helicopter, it occurred to Jack that we could flight test the concept at Langley. Bob Champine was the first test subject, and he was personally doubtful whether it was feasible, even as we walked out to the flight line, performed the preflight checks, and headed for the practice area. Control of the helicopter was transferred from the safety pilot to Champine, and, lo and behold, there's this loud exclamation over the intercom: 'This is a piece of cake!' From that point on, Champine couldn't find enough words of praise for on/off control. Without Reeder's inquiring thoughtfulness, this contribution, far a field of our normal focus, would not have been made."[3]
>
> Reeder's intense passion for analyzing aircraft behavior even carried over to times when he was not on research missions. Langley researcher Robert Huston recalled: "One time, Jack and I were relaxing in our seats while flying as passengers aboard a civil transport on a business trip, when all of the sudden during the flight Jack exclaimed 'There, did you feel that Dutch roll.'"[4]

Reeder also took it upon himself to mentor along the junior test pilots in Langley's Flight Research Division, establishing a sense of camaraderie and "brotherhood" among the pilots. He was also a staunch supporter of NASA's aeronautics programs and resented it when his research pilots were reassigned to tasks supporting the Space Program, which was still relatively in its infancy.[5]

Sam Morello, one of the leading researchers and managers of Langley's research efforts for civil transports remembered Jack:

> "When I came to work in flight research at Langley in 1965, Jack Reeder was 'God'. Not only the flight-test engineers, but also the rest of the pilots, showed great respect for Jack. As Chief Pilot and Head of Flight Operations, he was recognized throughout

the world as being one of the premier research test pilots, having flown an amazing variety of fixed-wing aircraft, helicopters, V/STOL aircraft, and even the Concorde. As a young, wet behind the ears, flight-test engineer, I hung on every word Jack said. He seemed to recognize my love for airplanes and flight, and decided to mentor me in the fine points of aircraft stability and control. If he was going out to do a check flight on one of the fixed-wing airplanes or helicopters, he would take me along to show me what the phugoid,*[1] short period, and dutch roll**[2] felt like. He would even let me pulse the control to initiate the short period, or push the rudder and stick all the way in opposite directions to start the Dutch roll. Jack made textbook knowledge come to life.

I was always amazed that after one of his flights to document the stability characteristics of a test airplane he would hand me his notes concerning the period, frequency, and decay times of the various stability characteristics of the airplane. Later I would get the plastic oscillography off the airplane and do the analysis. He was always right on the mark with his assessment. Some of the pilots and I thought Jack was rough when he flew airplanes. After looking back on it, I think it was Jack's way of really getting the sense or feel of the plane. He was always testing the airplane, even if he was flying us somewhere for a meeting he never flew just straight and level.

Jack was the first real visionary that I knew within the NASA culture. Until Jack showed us his vision of what we could achieve in the civil/commercial aviation world, we at Langley were mainly working military aircraft problems. Jack conceived the Ter-

---

**A phugoid or fugoid /ˈfjuːɡɔɪd/ is an aircraft motion where the vehicle pitches up and climbs, and then pitches down and descends, accompanied by speeding up and slowing down as it goes "uphill" and "downhill." This is one of the basic flight dynamics modes of an aircraft (others include short period, dutch roll, and spiral divergence), and a classic example of a negative feedback system.

2 * ** A Dutch Roll is a combination of rolling and yawing (coupled lateral/ directional) oscillations that normally occurs when the dihedral effects of an aircraft are more powerful than the directional stability. Usually dynamically stable but objectionable in an airplane because of the oscillatory nature. The damping of the oscillatory mode may be weak or strong depending on the properties of the particular aircraft.

If the aircraft has a right wing pushed down, the positive sideslip angle corrects the wing laterally before the nose is realigned with the relative wind. As the wing corrects the position, a lateral directional oscillation can occur resulting in the nose of the aircraft making a figure eight on the horizon as a result of two oscillations (roll and yaw), which, although of about the same magnitude, are out of phase with each other.

minal Configured Vehicle Program when most of the other top managers were skeptical of his dreams of how new technology and operating procedures could revolutionize civil aviation. He asked me to join his small team to put the program together, and I was extremely honored to join him. It was a tough job to convince Langley management and even harder to get the money from NASA Headquarters. No matter what happened in one of our many briefings at Headquarters, Jack was always positive, and kept telling us not to let the SOBs wear us down. He took us out to Boeing and got them excited about joining the effort. It was Jack's reputation that made that program happen, and started us down a long and successful journey."[6]

In his spare time, Jack enjoyed several interests. His wife Frances commented: "First and foremost, he enjoyed traveling back to the Upper Peninsula of Michigan, where he was born. He loved it up there. We eventually bought his Uncle's log cabin up there, located on the shore of Lake Superior. We would go up there for two weeks and then the next summer we would go up there for three weeks. I think one time we actually stayed up there for two months out of the summer."[7] Jack enjoyed traveling throughout the world and the Reeders particularly enjoyed traveling to New Zealand, Wales, Ireland, France, and Greece. Jack and his family enjoyed playing golf and the Reeders were members of the Jamestown/Newport News Country Club. The Reeder family also enjoyed playing tennis together. The family also spent time on the water in a boat that Jack owned. He learned how to water-ski, and became quite proficient at it. Unfortunately, maintenance and cost issues caused him to eventually sell the boat. Jack was a member of the Newport News Yacht Club and his daughters thoroughly enjoyed going for swims in the Club's swimming facilities. Jack and Frances also enjoyed going to dinners, dances, and parties hosted by the Club. Jack also enjoyed taking his daughters for scenic drives in the family car, and to trips to the Langley Research Center Flight Hangar, the Newport News International Airport (previously known as "Patrick Henry International Airport"), and other destinations, primarily to watch airplanes taking off and landing, or to make flights together in helicopters or GA airplanes. Jack also enjoyed flying his own personal Cessna and later a restored Monocoupe.

One incident that spoke volumes of Jack's legendary career happened in the early 1970s and was shared by many of his friends. On that occasion, Jack had joined a group of Langley researchers for a tour of the Paul E. Garber Preservation, Restoration, and Storage Facility of the Smithsonian Museum, located in Suitland, Maryland. In preparation for a tour of several hangar buildings filled with aircraft artifacts, the Langley group joined a larger contingent of tourists, to be led by a noted aviation writer who had volunteered to serve as a tour guide that day.

At the first hangar, the tour guide opened the door, turned on the lights and began to point out the historically significant aircraft inside. Jack, being up front with a good viewing point, immediately blurted out "Look here! This is the XP-51 Mustang that I flew back at Langley in 1944. Let me show you the aileron modifications we made to lighten the stick forces!" After a significant lecture on other aspects of his XP-51 experiences, Jack turned and proclaimed "My gosh—look over in the corner at the Curtiss-Wright X-100 that I flew in 1960!" Once again, Jack gave an impromptu lecture on the history of the airplane and his assessments of it. By now, the crowd (and the tour guide) knew it had a real expert in its midst, and in subsequent stops at other storage hangars, the tour guide simply opened the door and asked Jack to address the airplanes within! After entertaining and educational lectures by Jack in front of other aircraft in storage at the time (Vertol VZ-2, Hiller HOE-1 Hornet, XC-35, etc.), the entire crowd gave Jack a loud round of applause and appreciation. They all knew they were with a special person and an American treasure, just as praiseworthy as the artifacts on display.

Alzheimer's Disease

In the summer of 1990, Jack was driving his car during a vacation to Michigan's Upper Peninsula, like he did most summers, when he lost control and his car veered off the road and struck a formation of birch trees. In the accident, Jack suffered severe head wounds that tragically hindered his short-term memory and recall capability. In fact, he could not recall if he had fallen asleep at the wheel, or blacked out from another cause. In 1992, Jack was diagnosed with the onset of Alzheimer's disease. Following the diagnosis, he resigned from his consultant positions.

The year 1992 proved to be bittersweet, for along with the diagnosis of Alzheimer's that year, Jack was inducted into the prestigious Michigan Aviation Hall of Fame in view of his monumental contributions to aviation. The Michigan Aviation Hall of Fame was organized in 1987 with objectives to (1) educate the public – particularly young people – about the history of aviation and the contributions of Michigan citizens to the development of worldwide aviation, (2) honor those citizens whose outstanding achievements have advanced aviation or aerospace in Michigan, the United States or the world, and (3) help perpetuate the ongoing contributions of Michigan citizens to the aviation community for decades to come. Jack joined other notable Michigan natives in the Hall of Fame including famous airplane designers Clarence "Kelly" Johnson, Edward Heinemann, William Boeing, Sr., William Powell Lear, and Harry J. Hillaker. In the 1992 ceremony, one of his heroes, Charles A. Lindbergh, accompanied Jack's enshrinement. Frances Reeder remembers the excitement of the enshrinement event. "We met Charles Lindbergh's grandson and his wife."[8]

The progression of Alzheimer's ravaged Jack during the mid 1990s, and on May 23, 1999, four days shy of his eighty-third birthday, he succumbed to the effects of the disease. He left behind his beloved wife Frances, daughters Shirley and Carol, and four grandchildren. He was laid to rest in the Peninsula Memorial Park Cemetery in Newport News, Virginia.

Jack Reeder's restored Monocoupe.
Jack Reeder via NASA Langley Research Center

Virginia Aviation Hall of Fame

In November 2005, Jack Reeder was inducted posthumously into the Virginia Aviation Hall of Fame. One of the most successful projects sponsored by the Virginia Aeronautical Historical Society, the Hall of Fame was created to honor Virginians who have made significant contributions to the development of aviation. The citation for his induction states:

> *"Reeder was a test pilot who became the first National Advisory Committee for Aeronautics helicopter test pilot. He started working for NACA after he graduated from the University of Michigan in 1938. His first assignment was working with wind-tunnel staff at Langley Memorial Laboratory. The following year he received his private pilot's license. In 1942, Reeder took NACA in-house flight training, then transferred to the Flight Operations Branch. There, he was a test pilot for military fighters and bombers. In 1944, he became NACA's first helicopter test pilot. He is known for his pioneering work establishing basic flying qualities for helicopters and vertical and short takeoff planes. In the 1960s, he flew and evaluated the forerunner of the Harrier jet vertical-take-off fighter. In 42 years, Reeder flew 235 different types of aircraft including 38 jets, 40 fighters, 16 rotary wing planes and 8 vertical take-off aircraft."*

The extraordinary career and personal life of John P. "Jack" Reeder can be placed at the leading edge of aviation notables. A fine gentleman who only wanted to pursue the flame that had burned within him as a young boy accomplished so much, in such a low-key manner. He will long be remembered as one of the central figures in the Golden Years of aeronautical accomplishments for the NACA and NASA.

Old friends meet again. Forty-eight years after his first flight tests in the XP-51, Jack Reeder stands on the wing of the airplane at the Experimental Aircraft Association's Flyin of 1992 at Oshkosh, Wisconsin. The restored XP-51 is now on display at the EAA's Air Venture Museum in Oshkosh.

Jack Reeder

Chapter Nine Notes

1. Interview with Lee Person (April 11, 2006). Yorktown, Va.

2. Interview with Robert Tapscott (March 29, 2006). Yorktown, Va.

3. Email and Telephone interview with John Garren (August 3, 2006).

4. Phone interview with Robert Huston (March 29, 2006). Yorktown, Va.

5. Interview with Lee Person (April 11, 2006). Yorktown, Va.

6. Email interview with Sam Morello (August 14, 2006).

7. Interview with Mrs. Frances Winder Reeder and Shirley Reeder Randall (March 20, 2006). Newport News, Va.

8. Ibid.

Appendices

Appendix A

Aircraft and Rotorcraft Piloted by John P. "Jack" Reeder

NACA/NASA Langley test pilot John P. "Jack" Reeder test flew 235 types of aircraft/rotorcraft. The following is a listing of those aircraft/rotorcraft:

Single Engine Propeller-Driven GA Aircraft

1. Franklin Glider (flown before start of NACA career)
2. Cub J-3 (flown before start of NACA career)
3. Taylorcraft (flown before start of NACA career)
4. Waco INF (flown before start of NACA career)
5. Cub J-4 (flown before start of NACA career)
6. Monocoupe (flown before start of NACA career)
7. Cub J-5 (flown before start of NACA career)
8. Ercoupe (flown before start of NACA career)
9. Cub J-2 (flown before start of NACA career)
10. Cub J-3 (with NACA alterations)
11. Ryan STA
12. Fairchild XR2K-1
13. Stinson SR-8E
14. Fairchild 24

15. Culver Q-14b
16. Aeronca Champion
17. Waco C
18. Luscombe 65
19. Stinson (150 and Voyager)
20. Fairchild PT-19
21. Cub
22. Stinson L-5E (quiet propeller configuration)
23. Beech 35 Bonanza
24. Cessna 190 and 195
25. Culver Model V
26. North American Aviation L-17B Navion
27. Cessna 170
28. Swift
29. Piper L-21
30. Piper Tri-Pacer
31. Piper Clipper
32. Cessna 182
33. Cessna 175
34. Cessna 150
35. Cessna 140
36. Cessna L-19A
37. Dornier DO-27
38. Commonwealth 185
39. Piper Vagabond
40. Roberston STOL
41. Wren 460 STOL
42. Piper Cherokee

43. Mooney 21
44. Lockheed Bushmaster
45. Cessna L-19
46. Helio Courier
47. Fairchild Heli-Porter
48. Champion Citabria
49. Schweitzer 222 Glider
50. Comanche 260
51. Beech Musketeer
52. Stearman PT-17
53. Cessna 172
54. Cessna Redhawk
55. American Yankee AA-1
56. Beech Sundowner
57. BD-4
58. Great Lakes 2T-1A2
59. Thorpe T-18
60. Piper Cherokee Arrow, T-tail
61. Schweizer 2-33 glider
62. Piper PA-12 on floats

Single Engine Propeller-Driven World War II Military Aircraft

1. Grumman XTBF-1 Torpedo Bomber
2. Brewster XSBA-1
3. North American Aviation AT-6 (Army Air Force) and SNJ (Navy)
4. Curtiss XP-42

5. Bell P-39D-1

6. Grumman F6F-3

7. Curtiss SB2C-1

8. Bell YP-39

9. Vought F4U-1

10. North American Aviation P-51B

11. Brewster F2A-2

12. Republic P-47C

13. Republic P-47D-5

14. North American Aviation XP-51

15. Vultee SNV-1

16. Bell P-63A-1

17. Vought F3A-1 and F4U-4

18. Supermarine Spitfire Mk. VII

19. Curtiss P-40F

20. North American Aviation P-51D

21. Grumman XF6F-4

22. Curtiss SB2C-3

23. Curtiss SC-1

24. Republic P-47D-30 and D-28

25. Grumman FM-2

26. Grumman F8F-1 and F8F-2 prototype

27. North American Aviation P-51H

28. Douglas SBD-5

29. Republic P-47N

30. Bell L-39

Multi Engine Propeller-Driven World War II Military Aircraft

1. Douglas A-26B
2. North American Aviation B-25C
3. Consolidated B-24D
4. Boeing B-17G
5. Boeing B-29 (two types)
6. DeHavilland F-8 Mosquito

Post World War II Single Engine Propeller-Driven Military Aircraft

1. North American Aviation T-28A (Navy trainer)

Post World War II Multi Engine Propeller-Driven Military Aircraft

1. North American Aviation XF-82 and F-82b (Twin Mustang)

Multi Engine Propeller-Driven Transport Aircraft

1. Lockheed 12
2. Lockheed XC-35
3. Beech UC-45
4. Grumman JRF-5
5. Douglas C-47 and R4D
6. Grumman J4F Widgeon (original hull)

7. Grumman J4F Widgeon (modified hull)

8. Grumman J4F Widgeon (planing-tail hulls)

9. Cessna UC-78

10. Dehavilland Dove

11. Grumman G-73 Mallard

12. Lockheed Lodestar

13. Aerocommander

14. Grumman SA-16

15. Convair T-29B and C

16. Grumman Gulfstream I

17. DeHavilland Caribou (STOL aircraft)

18. Varsity (British aircraft)

19. Beech King Air

20. Beech 18 Tri-gear

21. Beech Queen Air BE-65

22. Cessna U-3A

23. DeHavilland DHC-6 Twin Otter (STOL aircraft)

24. Douglas C-54D

25. Lockheed Electra

26. Brequet 941 STOL

27. Piper Aztec E (GA design)

28. Rutan "Defiant" Prototype (GA design)

29. Beech B-80

Single Engine Military Jet Aircraft

1. Lockheed F-80A and B
2. Republic YF-84
3. North American Aviation F-86A
4. Grumman F9F-3 and F9F-2
5. Lockheed TV-2 and T-33A
6. Bell X-5
7. North American F-86D
8. Grumman F9F-6, -7
9. North American Aviation F-100 A & C
10. Convair YF-102
11. Chance Vought F8U-1
12. Grumman F11F-1
13. Hawker Hunter (two seat)
14. Handley Page 115
15. Lockheed TF-104G

Multi Engine Jet Aircraft

1. North American Aviation B-45
2. Boeing B-47A
3. Chance Vought F7U-1
4. McDonnell XF-88B (supersonic propeller research testbed)
5. McDonnell F2H-1
6. Douglas F3D-2
7. McDonnell F-101A

8. Cessna T-37A
9. Douglas DC-8
10. Lockheed Jetstar
11. Boeing 367-80 (STOL research using blown flap)
12. Boeing 367-80 (SST simulator research)
13. North American Aviation T-38A
14. Lear Jet 23
15. Boeing 727
16. Grumman Gulfstream II
17. Boeing 737
18. North American Aviation Sabreliner 75
19. Boeing 747
20. Boeing 737 (TCV aircraft)
21. Lockheed L-1011-500 Tri-Star
22. Concorde

V/STOL Propeller-Driven Aircraft

1. Vertol VZ-2 (tilt-wing prop)
2. Bell XV-3 (tilt-rotor)
3. Doak VZ-4 (tilt-duct)
4. Curtiss X-100 (tilt-prop)
5. Canadair CL-84 (tilt-wing)

V/STOL Jet Powered Aircraft

1. Short SC.1 (lift-cruise)
2. Bell X-14 (lift-cruise)
3. Hawker P.1127 (Harrier Prototype, vectored thrust)

Helicopters

1. Sikorsky HNS-1 and YR-4B
2. Sikorsky HOS-1
3. Bell 47
4. Piasecki PV-3
5. Teicher "Hummingbird"
6. Bendix Co-axial "Whirlaway"
7. Sikorsky HO3S-1
8. Hiller 360
9. Hiller UH-5
10. Bell H-13B
11. Sikorsky XHJS-1
12. Piasecki XHJP-1
13. Kaman K-190
14. Sikorsky S-52
15. Kaman K-225
16. Piasecki HRP-1
17. Piasecki HUP-1
18. Sikorsky XHO3S-2
19. Hiller Hornet (ram jet tipped blade testbed)
20. Piasecki HRP-2
21. Hiller HTE-1
22. Sikorsky HRS-1 and HRS-3
23. Bell XHSL-1 (tandem rotor testbed)
24. LeDjinn (French jet tipped blade testbed)
25. Bristol 171 (British helicopter)
26. Bristol 173 (tandem rotor helicopter)

27. Sikorsky HSS-1
28. Cessna CH-1
29. Vertol H-21
30. Bell 47J
31. Hiller YH-32 (ram jet tipped blade testbed)
32. Alouette II (French turbine testbed)
33. Sikorsky H-37A & HR2S-1
34. Bell YH-40 and 204B
35. Cessna YH-41 and CH-1C
36. Bell HTL-7
37. Vertol 107
38. Lockheed CL-475 (hingeless rotor testbed, JPR test flew two versions)
39. Hughes 269A
40. Kellet KD-1A Autogiro
41. Bell H-13 (hingeless rotor)
42. Hiller H-23D
43. Hiller 12L (prototype)
44. YROE-1
45. Lockheed XH-51A, XH-51N and Model 286 (hingeless rotor testbeds)
46. Sikorsky S-62 (HH-52A)
47. Sikorsky S-61R (CH-3C)
48. Sikorsky S-61N
49. Sikorsky HSS-2
50. Bell Sioux Scout (Cobra prototype)
51. Teicher Hummingbird (basic control systems)
52. Bell OH-4A
53. Kaman H-43

54. Piasecki HUP-1(variable stability studies at Princeton)
55. Vertol YHC-1A (Langley Research Center variable stability studies)
56. Vertol-Boelkow 105 (German hingeless rotor testbed)
57. Bell OH-58A
58. Sikorsky CH-54B
59. Bell AH-1E
60. CH-47
61. Army OH-58
62. Sikorsky S-76

Appendix B

Bibliography of John P. "Jack" Reeder's Published Papers

NACA/NASA Langley test pilot John P. "Jack" Reeder was the author or co-author of 69 technical publications or presentations. A listing of these works follows:

Dearborn, Clinton H., Silverstein, Abe, and Reeder, John P.: Tests of XP-40 Airplane in NACA Full-Scale Tunnel. Memorandum Report for Army. May 16, 1939.

Goett, Harry J., and Reeder, John P.: Effects of Elevator Nose Shape, Gap, Balance, and Tabs on the Aerodynamic Characteristics of a Horizontal Tail Surface. NACA TR 675, 1939.

Reeder, John P., and Nelson, William J.: Tests of the XP-39B Airplane in the NACA Full-Scale Wind Tunnel. Memorandum Report for Army. March 16, 1940.

Wilson, Herbert A., Jr., and Reeder, John P.: Engine Cooling and Stability Tests of the XSO3C-1 Airplane in the Full-Scale Wind Tunnel. Memorandum Report. January 8, 1941.

Wilson, Herbert A., Jr., and Reeder, John P.: Engine Cooling and Clean-Up Tests of the A-20A Airplane in the NACA Full-Scale Wind Tunnel. Memorandum Report for Army. June 12, 1941.

Reeder, John P., and Preston, G. Merritt: Full-Scale Wind-Tunnel Tests of the General Motors Aerial Torpedo. Memorandum Report for Army. October 29, 1941.

Reeder, John P., and Brewer, Gerald W.: NACA Full-Scale Wind-Tunnel Tests of Vought-Sikorsky V-173 Airplane. Memorandum Report for Navy. April 28, 1942.

Reeder, John P., and Biebel, William J.: Tests of Grumman XTBF-1 Airplane in the NACA Full-Scale Tunnel. Memroandum Report for Navy. October 21, 1942.

Reeder, John P., and Crane, Harold L.: Flight Tests of Various Tail Modifications on the Brewster XSBA-1 Airplane. III-Measurements of Flying Qualities with Tail Configuration 3. NACA RMR for Navy (WR L-599). July 12, 1944.

White, M.D., and Reeder, J. P.: Effect of Wing-Tip Slots on the Stalling and Aileron Control Characteristics of a Curtiss SB2C-1 Airplane. NACA MR L4K13 RMR for Navy. November 13, 1944.

Williams, Walter C., and Reeder, John P.: Flight Measurements of the Flying Qualities of an F6F-3 Airplane (BuAer No. 04776). I – Longitudinal Stability and Control. NACA RMR for Navy. February 13, 1945.

Williams, Walter C., and Reeder, John P.: Flight Measurements of the Flying Qualities of an F6F-3 Airplane (BuAer No. 04776). II – Lateral and Directional Stability and Control. NACA MR L5B13a RMR for Navy. February 13, 1945.

Williams, Walter C., and Reeder, John P.: Flight Measurements of the Flying Qualities of an F6F-3 Airplane (BuAer No. 04776). III – Stalling Characteristics. NACA MR L5B13b RMR for Navy. February 13, 1945.

White, Maurice D., and Reeder, John P.: Flight Investigation of Modifications to Improve the Elevator Control-Force Characteristics of the Curtiss SB2C-1C Airplane in Maneuvers – TED No. NACA 2333. NACA MR L5DO4a RMR for Navy. April 16, 1945.

Hunter, Paul A., and Reeder, John P.: Flight Measurements to Determine Effect of a Spring-Loaded Tab on Longitudinal

Stability of an Airplane. NACA ARR No. L5I20 (WR L-210). NACA MR L5G26a RMR for Navy. February 1946.

Danforth, Edward C. B. III, and Reeder, John P.: Flight Measurements of Internal Cockpit Pressures in Several Fighter-Type Airplanes. NACA TN 1173. February 1947.

Talmage, Donald B., and Reeder, John P.: Flight Measurements of the Handling Characteristics of a C-54D Airplane (AAF No. 42-72713) with Particular Reference to the Blind Landing Approach Condition. NACA RM L7L17a. 1947.

Sjoberg, S. A., and Reeder, John P.: Flight Measurements of the Lateral and Directional Stability and Control Characteristics of an Airplane Having a 35° Sweptback Wing with 40-Percent-Span Slots and a Comparison with Wind-Tunnel Data. NACA TN 1511. January 1948.

Kraft, C. C. Jr., and Reeder, J. P.: Measurements of the Lateral and Directional Stability and Control Characteristics of a P-51H Airplane (AAF No. 44-64164). NACA RM SL7L11 RM for AAF AirMatCom. January 27, 1948.

Crane, Harold L., and Reeder, John P.: Flight Measurements of Lateral and Directional Stability and Control Characteristics of the Grumman F8F-1 Airplane (TED NACA 2379). NACA RM SL7L31 for Navy. January 29, 1948.

Kraft, C. C. Jr., Goranson, R. F., and Reeder, John P.: Measurements of Flying Qualities of an F-47D-30 Airplane to Determine Longitudinal Stability and Control and Stalling Characteristics. NACA TN 2899 (Issued February 1953). NACA RM SL8A06 (Issued February 18, 1948).

Kraft, C. C. Jr., and Reeder, J. P.: Measurements of the Longitudinal Stability and Control and Stalling Characteristics of a North American P-51H Airplane (AAF No. 4-64164). NACA RM S18324, RM for USAF AirMatCom. March 23, 1948.

Gustafson, F. B., and Reeder, J. P.: Helicopter Stability. NACA RM L7K04, April 12, 1948.

Reeder, John P., and Gustafson, F. B.: Notes on the Flying Qualities of Helicopters. Presented at the American Helicopter Society Meeting April 22-24, 1948. (Proceedings of the Fourth Annual Forum, April 22-24, 1948, American Helicopter Society).

Sjoberg, S. A., and Reeder, J. P.: Flight Measurements of the Longitudinal Stability, Stalling, and Lift Characteristics of an Airplane Having a 35° Sweptback Wing Without Slots and With 40-Percent-Span Slots and a Comparison with Wind-Tunnel Data. NACA TN 1679, August 1948.

Assadourian, Arthur, and Reeder, John P.: Flight Measurements of the Longitudinal Stability and Control Characteristics of the Grumman F8F-1 Airplane – TED No. NACA 2379. NACA RM S18H27 RM for Navy. September 3, 1948.

Sjoberg, S. A., and Reeder, J. P.: Flight Measurements of the Stability, Control, and Stalling Characteristics of an Airplane Having a 35° Sweptback Wing Without Slots and with 80-Percent-Span Slots and a Comparison with Wind-Tunnel Data. NACA TN 1743, November 1948.

Talmage, Donald B., and Reeder, John P.: The Effects of Friction in the Control System on the Handling Qualities of a C-54D Airplane. NACA RM L8G30a, November 8, 1948.

Reeder, John P., and Gustafson, F. B.: On the Flying Qualities of Helicopters. NACA TN 1799, January 1949.

Talmage, Donald B., and Reeder, John P.: Lateral and Directional Stability and Control Characteristics of a C-54D Airplane. NACA RM L8K30, March 24, 1949.

Reeder, John P., and Haig, Chester R. Jr.: Some Tests of the Longitudinal Stability and Control of an H-13B Helicopter in Forward Flight. NACA RM L9E25a, August 1, 1949.

Gustafson, F. B., Amer, Kenneth B., Haig, C. R., and Reeder, J. P.: Longitudinal Flying Qualities of Several Single-Rotor Helicopters in Forward Flight. NACA TN 1983, November 1949.

Talmage, Donald B., Reeder, John P., and Matthews, Ruth G.: Flight Investigation of Longitudinal Stability and Control Characteristics and Stalling Characteristics of a C-54D Airplane. NACA RM L9L21, May 12, 1950.

Reeder, John P.: Helicopter Flight Research at NACA, Langley. Presented at Section Meeting of American Helicopter Society, November 15, 1951.

Reeder, John P., and Whitten, James B.: Some Effects of Varying the Damping in Pitch and Roll on the Flying Qualities of a Small Single-Rotor Helicopter. NACA TN 2459, January 1952.

Crim, Almer D., Reeder, John P., and Whitten, James B.: Initial Results of Instrument-Flying Trials Conducted in a Single-Rotor Helicopter. NACA Report 1137 (Issued as NACA TN 2721, June 1952).

Crim, Almer D. , Reeder, John P., and Whitten, James B.: Instrument-Flight Results Obtained with a Combined-Signal Flight Indicator Modified for Helicopter Use. NACA TN 2761, August 1952.

Reeder, John P., and Gustafson, Frederic B.: Flying Qualities of Tandem-Rotor Helicopters. Published in Aero Digest, Vol. 66, No. 5, May 1953.

Reeder, John P., and Gustafson, F. B.: Flying-Qualities Criteria for General-Purpose Helicopters. NACA Conference on Helicopters (A Compilation of Papers Presented), May 12-13, 1954.

Crim, Almer D., Whitten, James D., and Reeder, John P.: An Investigation of the Effect of Damping on Precision Maneuvers and Instrument Flight. NACA Conference on Helicopters (A Compilation of Papers Presented), May 12-13, 1954.

Reeder, John P., and Whitten, James B.: Helicopter Handling Qualities in Contact and Instrument Flight. NACA Conference on Some Problems of Aircraft Operation, November 17-18, 1954.

Reeder, John P.: Notes on Helicopter Flight Research. Presented to Flight Test Panel of AGARD, Paris, France, November 29-December 4, 1954.

Reeder, John P., and Tapscott, Robert J.: Note on Hovering Turns with Tandem Helicopters. NACA RM L55G21, September 15, 1955.

Whitten, James B., Reeder, John P., and Crim, Almer D.: Helicopter Instrument Flight and Precision Maneuvers as Affected by Changes in Damping in Roll, Pitch, and Yaw. NACA TN 3537, November 1955.

Reeder, John P., and Whitten, James B.: Notes on Steep Instrument Approaches in a Helicopter. Proceedings of the 12th Annual National Forum of American Helicopter Society, Washington, May 2-5, 1956.

Brown, B. P., and Reeder, J. P.: Some Effects of Valve Friction and Stick Friction on Control Quality in a Helicopter with Hydraulic-Power Control Systems. NACA TN 4004, May 1957.

Reeder, John P.: The Effect of Lift-Drag Ratio and Speed on the Ability to Position a Gliding Aircraft for a Landing on a 5,000-Foot Runway. NASA Memo 3-12-59L, April 1959.

Langley Research Center Staff: The V/STOL Transport. "Operational Aspects," by John P. Reeder. A Technical Summary Prepared for the Port of New York Authority , April 1960. NASA CC-L-1054 (Published as TN D-624, with the title "A Preliminary Study of V/STOL Transport Aircraft and Bibliography of NASA Research in the VTOL-STOL Field." Nov. 1960.

Mallick, Donald L., and Reeder, John P.: Flight Evaluation of Several Spring Force Gradients and a Bobweight in the Cyclic-Power-Control System of a Light Helicopter. NASA TN D-537, October 1960.

Reeder, John P.: Flight Research with a Tilt-Wing VTOL Test-Bed Aircraft. Presented at Society of Experimental Test Pilots 1960 Symposium, Los Angeles, California, October 8, 1960.

Reeder, John P.: Handling Qualities Experience with Several VTOL Research Aircraft. NASA Conference on V/STOL Aircraft, Langley Research Center, November 17-18, 1960.

Reeder, John P.: Flight Research with a Tilt-Wing VTOL Test-Bed Aircraft. Symposium Proceedings of Society of Experimental Test Pilots, 1960. Quarterly Review, Vol. 5, No. 2.

Reeder, John P.: Handling Qualities Experience with Several VTOL Research Aircraft. NASA TN D-735, January 18, 1961.

Wetmore, Joseph W., and Reeder, John P.: Aircraft Vortex Wakes in Relation to Terminal Operations. NASA TN D-1777 (Presented at the Symposium on Development of Analytical Models for Estimating Airport Capacity, California University, November 29-30, 1962).

Reeder, John P.: Operational Aspects of V/STOL Aircraft. Presented at DOD Symposium on V/STOL Aircraft, Kirtland AFB, New Mexico, April 23-24, 1963.

Kuhn, Richard E., Reeder, John P., and Alford, William J. Jr.: Jet V/STOL Tactical Aircraft. Reprint from Astronautics and Aerospace Engineering, June 1963, pages 38-43.

Reeder, John P., and Kolnick, Joseph J.: A Brief Study of Closed-Circuit Televisionfor Aircraft Landing. NASA TN D-2185, November 1963.

McKinney, M. O. Jr., Kuhn, R. E., and Reeder, J. P.: Aerodynamics and Flying Qualities of Jet V/STOL Airplanes. Presented at the SAE-ASME National Aeronautic Meeting, New York, April 27-30, 1964.

Garren, John F., Kelley, James R., Reeder, John P.: A Visual Flight Investigation of Hovering and Low Speed VTOL Contract Requirements. 1964.

Garren, John F., Kelley, James R., Reeder, John P.: Effects of Gross Changes in Static Directional Stability on V/STOL Handling Characteristics Based on a Flight Investigation. 1964.

Reeder, John P.: V/STOL Aircraft Operation in the Terminal Area. 1965.

Kelley, H. L.; Pegg, R. J.; Reeder, J. P.: Flight Investigation of the VZ-2 Tilt-Wing Aircraft with Full-Span Flap. NASA-TN-D-2680, March 1, 1965.

Garren, J. F., Jr.; Reeder, J. P.; Tapscott, R. J.: The Case For Inherent Stability Of Helicopters. NASA-TM-X-57798, Jan 1, 1966.

Reeder, John P.: V/STOL Terminal Area Instrument Flight Research. NASA-TM-X-60456; Air Transport Session of the 11th Annual Meeting of the Society of Experimental Test Pilots, Beverly Hills, CA, , September 28-30, 1967.

Reeder, John P.: What's Important in Simulation? Flight Safety Foundation, Annual International Air Safety Seminar, Anaheim, Calif., Oct. 8-11, 1968.

Kelley, Henry L.; Reeder, John P., Champine, Robert A.: Summary of a Flight-Test Evaluation of the CL-84 Tilt-Wing V/STOL Aircraft. 1969.

Recommendations for V/STOL Handling Qualities. AGARD Report 403, October 1962.

Reeder, John P.: Notes on Helicopter Flight Research. Presented to Flight Test Panel of AGARD, Paris, France, November 29-December 4, 1954.

Reeder, John P.: The Impact of V/STOL Aircraft on Instrument Weather Operations. Presented at the AGARD Flight Mechanics Panel Meeting on "All-Weather Operation" Munich, Germany, October 12-14, 1964.

Reeder, John P.; Tapscott, Robert J.; and Garren, John F., Jr.: The Case for Inherent Stability of Helicopters. Presented at the AGARD Meeting on Helicopter Developments, Paris, France, January 10-14, 1966.

Appendix C
Awards and Professional Association Memberships

Awards

1959 Octave Chanute Award of American Institute of Aeronautics and Astronautics

Fellow of Society of Experimental Test Pilots

Honorary Fellowship in American Helicopter Society

Recipient of 1964 Wright Brothers Medal of Society of Automotive Engineers

Tau Beta Pi, National Engineering Honor Society, University of Michigan

Burroughs Test Pilot Award for 1967 (Awarded by Flight Safety Foundation)

Honorary Member of Michigan Aviation Hall of Fame (Inducted in 1992)

Honorary Member of Virginia Aviation Hall of Fame (Inducted, posthumously, in November 2005)

Professional Associations

Society of Experimental Test Pilots (Fellow)

American Institute of Aeronautics and Astronautics (Assoc. Fellow)

American Helicopter Society (Honorary Fellowship)

Twirly Birds (Pioneer Helicopter Pilots)

Engineers Club of Virginia Peninsula

Torch Club

NASA Langley research pilots (from left to right) Lee Person, Dick Yenni, and Jack Reeder discuss a research project while seated in the aft cockpit of Langley's B-737 flying laboratory.

NASA Langley Research Center via Jack Reeder

About the Author

Mark Chambers is a contract Cultural Resource Specialist at the NASA Langley Research Center in Hampton, Virginia. He is the author of eight aviation history books, including two published by NASA (one of which he was a co-author with his father, Joseph). He has authored three titles published by Arcadia Publishing, including: Flight Research at NASA Langley Research Center, Naval Air Station Patuxent River, and NASA Kennedy Space Center. He can be reached at: markachambers@verizon.net .

Chambers, 49, is married to wife Lesa and has three children – daughter Caitlyn (age 16), son Patrick (age 5), and son Ryan (age 1 and ½). Mark is currently working on three books: In Service: Junkers Military Aircraft of World War II (The History Press Ltd. UK), Nakajima B5N "Kate" and B6N "Jill" Units (Combat Aircraft Series, Osprey Publishing), and Joint Base Langley Eustis (Images of Modern America, Arcadia Publishing). He is a native of Newport News, VA.

Chambers has won numerous awards with NASA for his past technical editing experience with Langley Research Center. These awards included NASA Group Achievement Awards with the NASA Engineering and Safety Center (NESC) and the Ares I-X Systems Engineering & Integration (SE&I) Office. He hopes to one day travel to Europe; visiting England, Ireland, Germany, and Italy. He enjoys dining out with his family at local restaurants in his home city of Newport News, Virginia.

www.ingramcontent.com/pod-product-compliance
Lightning Source LLC
Chambersburg PA
CBHW032106090426
42743CB00007B/250